How to watch birds

ROGER BARTON

Naturalist, NEWARK NEWS
President, New Jersey Audubon Society

McGraw-Hill Book Company, Inc.

NEW YORK TORONTO LONDON

QL
677
5
B37

HOW TO WATCH BIRDS

Copyright © 1955 by the McGraw-Hill Book Company, Inc.
All rights in this book are reserved. It may not be
used for dramatic, motion-, or talking-picture purposes
without written authorization from the holder of these
rights. Nor may the book or parts thereof be repro-
duced in any manner whatsoever without permission in
writing, except in the case of brief quotations embodied
in critical articles and reviews. For information,
address the McGraw-Hill Book Company, Inc., Trade
Department, 330 West 42d Street, New York 36, New York.

Library of Congress Catalog Card Number: 55-6146

Published by the McGraw-Hill Book Company, Inc.
Printed in the United States of America

Mc Clurg

3.50

May 31, 1956

to Priscilla

Contents

chapter 1 / What is a bird watcher?

Anyone can be a bird watcher. You don't need a badge or a membership card. You don't need to be athletic. You don't even need to have been born with a love of birds, for some people don't acquire this interest until they are past middle age.

It used to be that the person with binoculars was the butt of as much merriment as the man with a butterfly net. But that was half a century ago, and the thousands of bird watchers who followed Teddy Roosevelt have increased to the hundreds of thousands who follow Peterson and Pough.

How many bird watchers?

My guess is that there are close to 10,000,000 bird watchers in the United States today. By "bird watcher," I mean anyone who goes outdoors for the specific purpose of watching birds, or who supplies seed and suet to the feathered visitors at his kitchen window, or who takes more than a casual interest in their behavior.

This estimate is based upon several facts. One of them is my experience in writing a weekly column about birds for the *Newark Sunday News*. This newspaper has a circulation of 300,000, and approximately 90,000 of the readers, or 30 per cent, read my "Outdoors." Of course, I have been able to convert some casual readers into regular ones, and to stimulate the interest of others who may have had no previous interest in birds. Hence, I shall apply only a 22 per cent interest factor to the 45,900,000 readers of the nation's Sunday newspapers. This gives 10,000,000 as potential bird watchers.

Or consider the approximately 10,000,000 children who have been enrolled in the National Audubon Society's junior membership plan since it was launched in 1910. This program alone is said to be training half a million active bird watchers and all-around naturalists every school year. This activity is supplemented by that of the Scouts. There are 3,100,000 members of the Boy Scouts of America and 2,100,000 Girl Scouts of the U.S.A. Turnover is fast, as boys and girls mature and leave the movements. Both organizations include bird study as integral parts of their programs. I attribute my own first serious interest in birds to the scouting program.

Or look at the sale of books. Roger Tory Peterson's *A Field Guide to the Birds* had sold 200,000 copies by mid-1954, and his *A Field Guide to Western Birds* another 100,000 copies. Richard H. Pough's publishers said that some 400,000 copies of his *Audubon Bird Guide* and *Audubon Water Bird Guide* had been distributed. This makes 700,000 copies of field guides by two authors alone, and while there is some duplication in ownership, it is also true that there are other guides and many reference books that are often used instead. Multiply the sales of basic bird books by the proportion of persons who are interested in birds but lack books, and you will again get several million bird watchers.

Why interest has increased

Probably the number of bird watchers of both the casual and the serious kind has doubled or tripled since the last war. The modern trend toward country living and activity has stimulated this growth. Moreover, Americans are awakening to the need for conserving their natural resources, and they realize the critical part that birds play in their national economy.

The high cost of living in the postwar world has no doubt also accelerated interest in a hobby that is inexpensive. For serious work a pair of binoculars is necessary, but this is a single expense for an item that will last a lifetime. I have had my 12-power binoculars for twenty-two years, and they seem good for another like period, although it cost ten dollars recently to have them cleaned. Birders may travel long distances in pursuit of especially interesting species, but millions find adequate pleasure in the winged visitors to their own back yards. Members of the National Audubon Society say they spend an average of $336 a year in pursuit of their nature interests.

It was predicted during the last war that there would be an upsurge of interest in simple outdoor activities once hostilities had ceased. The audiences of a thousand and more persons that are attracted to lectures and films about birds offered in many cities of the country are visible manifestations of this trend. I have seen 750 persons at a bird lecture in as remote a spot as Cape May. This growth of interest may have resulted partly from the fact that wars and other periods of strain breed reactions that lead people to seek simpler, less hectic pursuits. Even during the war I had the experience of leading two bird walks for military personnel and their wives who were living at one Army post where I was stationed. I recall vividly the intense interest they derived from the experience, even though most of them hardly knew one bird from another. In later years, at least three of them became confirmed bird watchers. Bird study brings relaxation, and it is a refreshing change from modern business pursuits. Roger Tory Peterson maintains that Americans are taking up bird watching in astounding numbers as an "antidote for the disillusionment of the postwar world." As one who heard too many activities after the first world war also attributed to postwar disillusionment, I am a bit dubious about this conclusion. But I do agree with his statement that the recent increase in bird watching is "a return to reality rather than an escape from it," because birds are beautiful, natural, and relatively simple creatures, and bird watching is generally done without ulterior motives.

Sex and stamina

The potential bird watcher need not feel that it is necessary to qualify by either sex or stamina for this avocation. An unpublished market study conducted by *Audubon Magazine* shows that 54 per cent of its readers are female and 46 per cent male. Their ages are distributed as follows:

Less than 21	5 per cent
21 to 40	18 per cent
40 to 60	46 per cent
More than 60	31 per cent

All members of the National Audubon Society receive the magazine, and these bird watchers are sufficiently representative of their kind. The chief occupation among them is housewife; next in number, in descending order, are teacher, professional, retired, engineer, executive, physician, student, mechanic, merchant, farmer, lawyer, and dentist.

I have estimated that two-thirds of my readers among *Newark News* subscribers are mature women who are housewives. At least, that is the complexion of my correspondence. It has been my observation that more boys than girls are interested in birds, and that boys tend to retain this interest in later life. Women, as a whole, do not appear to become active bird watchers until they are married and relieved after the passage of years of some of the more pressing duties of rearing a family. It is possible that women, being home much of the day and spending much of their time in the kitchen, naturally develop an interest in birds because the creatures are right outside their windows. The slight effort that is needed for the construction of a simple feeding tray and the dispensing of seed adds greatly to the interest of those who are at home.

But whichever your sex, you do not have to be athletic to become a competent bird watcher. Some kinds of bird watching demand a bit of stamina, such as the Big Days in the May migrations, when some enthusiasts spend a full twenty-four hours in the field in an effort to compile a long list of birds. Such full days sometimes produce 150 to 170 species, and obviously demand a proportionate expenditure of strength and energy. Or take C. L. Broley, the man who bands eagles. He is almost seventy-five years old, and has to possess considerable power and agility to climb the lofty trees in which the birds nest and to cope with the tough creatures themselves.

For the most part, however, the only exercise demanded by bird watching is leisurely walking, for so much time is spent observing birds along the path that not a great number of miles can be traversed. Moreover, increasing attention is being given these days to ecological studies rather than to the compiling of long lists of species or the pursuit of rarities. Serious study is being devoted to the relation of birds to their environment, such as their use of nesting materials, their struggles with one another for rights to certain territories, and variations in their feeding habits. Such studies require thought and research, but not a great deal of physical activity.

Bird watching as a boy

My own bird watching started forty-three years ago when I was a boy of seven living in the rural country that then existed in Shades Valley near Birmingham, Alabama. Every morning when I went out to the barn I found a covey of quail under the carriage. A farmer down the road had a flower garden that seemed thronged with hummingbirds. And at night, in addition to the great choruses of frogs, I heard the calls of the chuck-will's-widow. Next we lived in North Carolina, where I remember how common the red-headed woodpeckers were, and what a fine target they made for other boys' slingshots.

My interest in birds grew when we moved to Brooklyn and took a place near Prospect Park. I was nine years old then, and used to get up early so I could spend an hour or so in the park before school. There were ducks in the lake, grackles on the lawns, warblers in the terminal foliage of trees, and woodpeckers on their trunks. I also found it fun to visit the zoo when the animals had no other visitors.

When I was twelve years old my family moved to New Jersey. Our house was at the edge of town, only a short distance from the Passaic River and on the edge of wide fields and fresh-water marshes.

I had no books to help me identify the birds I saw; I relied chiefly on the bird cards that were included as premiums in packs of cigarettes. I found these cards more confusing than helpful, however, because they showed wood thrushes with red breasts, bluebirds with strangely variegated colors, and other birds painted to be artistic rather than authentic. I lacked field glasses, too, but was agile enough to creep close to most of the birds, the only species that gave me much trouble being the warblers that fed high in the crowns of trees. My ambition then was to write another *Natural History of Selborne*, with the New Jersey scene as my theme, and I kept a bird diary and notes about the first and last dates I saw various species.

Bird watchers at home

For purposes of easy classification, bird watchers may be grouped into those who stay at home, those who go afield, bird banders, and professionals. Of course, the terms are not mutually exclusive, but attempt rather to define the sphere of one's main activity.

FEEDING STATION. Undoubtedly the greatest bird-watching activity that is carried on at home is that centered in feeding stations. These stations can be simple trays fastened to window ledges or the most elaborate devices of wood and glass offered by the mail-order merchants. Feeding stations include areas on the ground where feed is scattered, bird baths and pools, brush piles built for the birds' protection in stormy weather, and suet sticks hung from the limbs of trees.

This type of bird watching is highly satisfactory. It furnishes intimate views of the birds' colors and forms and of their behavior while feeding. It serves the additional useful purpose of contributing to the food supply that supports the bird population in the watcher's neighborhood. If the feeding is done regularly, it helps this population to increase.

One of the most inspiring stories of feeding-station operation is Ada Clapham Govan's *Wings at My Window*. Mrs. Govan was almost a cripple when she began to feed birds, undertaking this activity partly to take her mind off her troubles. She soon found that an amazing variety and number of birds came to her simple feeders, and that her success attracted bird watchers from a wide area. She then began to write a column about birds for a Boston newspaper, and later wrote her book, which has been bought by more than 28,000 persons.

Feeding-station operators who are members of one club in my state are organized into a kind of intelligence network. When one of the sixty-five operators discovers an interesting bird at her feeder, she notifies the rest. These operators participate in certain group activities as well. For instance, in the first week of each winter month they count the birds in their areas. These modest censuses, conducted year after year, have provided an excellent idea of regional bird population and its fluctuation.

Recently I enlisted the readers of my column in a cooperative effort to determine the order in which birds arrived each day at their stations and the specific times that they appeared. They established the fact that the cardinal was the first bird to appear in winter, that it was followed within a few minutes by the junco and sparrows. They also agreed that the cardinal came approximately half an hour before sunrise, and was also one of the last birds to feed in the afternoon. There are many other projects in which feeding-station operators can cooperate to produce worthwhile information.

Those who wish to know more about attracting birds to their yards will find the following chapters of particular interest: Chapter 4, "What to Feed Birds"; Chapter 5, "Bird Baths and Feeders"; Chapter 6, "Nesting Boxes and Shelters "; Chapter 7, "Plantings That Attract Birds."

Photography is another activity in which station operators engage, although their sphere of activity may extend far beyond their back yards. This subject will be discussed in Chapter 15, "Photographing Birds." Some bird watchers take pictures merely for their records; others have as much interest in photography as they do in birds, or more, and seek photographs that are artistic rather than documentary. Some 69 per cent of National Audubon members use a camera, and spend an average of $88.17 a year on photographic supplies.

I spend most of my time on week ends either watching birds or pounding my typewriter. I find I can do both at the same time by setting up a camera in my study with the lens focused on the feeding tray that is fastened to the window. I run a stout thread from the trigger of the camera to the typewriter. By keeping a peripheral glance on the window as I work, I can merely pull the thread when a cardinal, nuthatch, or other interesting visitor arrives, taking its picture without disturbing either of us.

YARD LISTS. It is fun to keep lists of birds observed in or from one's own yard. You can watch this list grow from year to year, and compare it with similar lists kept by other bird watchers. You can include any bird that you see or hear from your yard, as well as those actually in it. If you hear a passing killdeer's notes in the night or see a flock of Canada geese overhead, it is all right to include these species in your list. Of course, the birds that actually rest or feed in your yard will constitute the greatest number.

One of my correspondents is a girl now in her twenties who has been a bedridden victim of polio since she was a small child. She can get out of bed only an hour a day, so most of her bird watching is from her bedroom window. Until 1950 she lived in a house that was situated near a marsh and had a yard with a small stream running through it. In the three years between 1947 and 1950 this crippled girl observed 135 species of birds in her yard. In the latter year her family moved to a more suburban section, where her yard measures only 40 by 100 feet. Even there she has been able to find 50 species of birds. Her name is Dorothy Constance Pallas, and she and Carroll Lane Fenton have just written a book called *Birds and Their World* (1954).

It is possible for anyone to compile a list of 75 birds or so just from his yard. One correspondent of mine in a nearby town has seen 115. His yard also enjoys the advantage of a small brook.

Another example is a man in Collingswood who has developed his yard into a natural haven for birds and other wildlife. One fall he was visited by 15 species of warblers. He has seen 83 kinds of birds within his yard, and another 18 flying overhead. Ten birds nest in his yard. Included in his count are a woodcock and a saw-whet owl.

A woman who lives in Doylestown, Pennsylvania, had 15 species of birds in her yard on November 14 one year. Among them were a Carolina wren, a hairy woodpecker, and a myrtle warbler.

Another woman, in Rumson, has snowy egrets roosting on her property, and has seen a mockingbird and black-billed and yellow-billed cuckoos in the trees on her place. She keeps feeders and suet holders in operation at all times, and has enjoyed watching broods of various species, among them a family of wood pewees.

WATCHING THE MOON. Stay-at-home bird watchers can be as successful in watching lunar migrations as anyone else. This is a form of bird watching that has gained in popularity since the war. It consists of watching the full moon in the fall, especially in September and October, and observing the birds that pass over the silver disk. This activity has been conducted on a more or less formal basis by bird enthusiasts all over the United States and in Mexico and Puerto Rico. The results have been sent to Louisiana State University, which has coordinated the activity and correlated the findings. A great deal has been discovered about the routes birds take at night, the times they fly, the heights and directions they take, and whether they fly singly or in flocks. A great deal more has to be ascertained.

All you have to do is sit in your yard and watch the moon. A 20-power telescope is best for this kind of bird watching, but binoculars will serve. I have seen as many as 200 birds an hour pass over the face of the moon from a vantage point in my own back yard. The birds go over singly at night, and you can identify some as ducks or geese or herons or even swallows. This is a fascinating business, made more interesting by the weird background of the moon with its mysterious valleys and craters. Chapter 12, "Bird Watching at Night," discusses this subject in detail.

NESTING STUDIES. There are innumerable studies that you can make without going outside of your own yard. You can study how birds nest, for instance. How many species nest in a specific area, and does more than one pair of a species nest there? At what times do birds build their nests, when are the eggs hatched, when do the young leave the nest, how many broods are there? These and other questions make fascinating subjects to explore. The use of nesting materials is of especial interest, and bird watchers can experiment by putting out various materials, such as pieces of colored string, wisps of cotton, piles of straw, to see how they are utilized by the birds.

Mrs. Margaret Nice, whose life history of the song sparrow is the definitive work on this subject, began her study when she was a housewife in Ohio making only casual observations of the birds in her own yard. Her interest deepened, and her work was concluded largely upon the basis of data gathered around her own property.

What you can do to encourage more birds to nest around your house is told in Chapter 6, "Nesting Boxes and Shelters." If you become interested in studying nests after the birds have finished with them, you will find that Chapter 14, "Collecting Old Nests," offers some suggestions.

Bird watchers afield

However, many people want to see what life is like beyond the confines of their own homes. These bird watchers may be classified roughly as casual walkers, bird-club members, and professionals. Bird watchers like to go afield in pursuit of the subjects of their interest, and members of the National Audubon Society travel an average of 2,306 miles a year in pursuit of bird and other nature interests. For a further discussion of this subject see Chapter 11, "Fun on Field Trips."

CASUAL WALKERS. The casual walkers are the people—and they often include family groups—who explore the bird life in their own vicinity. It may be a park that holds chief interest for them, and sometimes the parks are excellent. Central Park in New York

City has afforded 225 species, and its Ramble is a section not far from the Metropolitan Museum that attracts bird watchers from a wide area.

I was a bird watcher for thirty years before I joined any bird club. I am still continually finding new places to walk in the region where I live. Sometimes these places are exceptionally good for birds, and often they are quite unknown to other bird watchers. I have found especially productive the two parks maintained by the county in my neighborhood, but there are also two airports that produce horned larks, snow buntings, and Lapland longspurs in season, and wonderful fresh-water marshes where there are rails, gallinules, and bitterns. These marshes are traversed by transmission lines of two electric light and power companies, and to maintain these lines the companies have built elevated boardwalks beneath them. These boardwalks are ideal for bird watchers, enabling them to penetrate the depths of the swamp without getting wet.

BIRD-CLUB MEMBERS. The watcher who is a member of a bird club gains several advantages. He is able to participate in organized activities, such as field trips and lectures. When he goes on field trips he may visit swamps, reservoirs, beaches, and other good birding areas that were unknown to him previously. Then, if he wishes later to visit these spots by himself, he can readily find them. He also learns much from associating with other bird watchers, who make available to him their varied experiences and funds of information. He also hears from his fellow club members what birds he can expect to see in different places and what rarities are about. The human relationships developed are enriching, for the clubs bring together people who have similar interests and temperaments. Finally, by joining such groups the individual bird watcher can lend his support to conservation programs whose accomplishment is possible only through concerted effort.

There are many different types of associations for bird watchers. There are the great national organizations—for instance, the National Audubon Society and the Wilson Ornithological Club. These groups have only one meeting a year for members, but they issue periodicals and carry much weight in national programs for conservation. Then there are the regional groups, such as the Massachusetts Audubon Society, the New Jersey Audubon Society, and other state-wide bodies. Their membership runs from a few hundred to several thousand, and they usually have a program of field trips for their members, conduct annual meetings, issue magazines or other periodicals, and also engage in conservation programs but on a state-wide basis.

Finally, there are the numerous local bird clubs, generally centered in a particular community. There is the Montclair Bird Club, for instance, the Summit Nature Club, the Ridgewood Audubon Society. Members of these clubs enjoy a program of field trips and lectures, associate with their neighbors, and have the benefit of local field notes often published by their group. Membership in any of these clubs, from the national to the local level, seldom costs more than three to five dollars a year.

You will find a list of bird clubs and a discussion of their advantages in Chapter 16, "Why Not Join a Bird Club?"

Bird banders

Bird banders are bird watchers of a very special kind. There are only some two thousand in the United States, and they have to qualify for their work by the endorsement of well-known ornithologists and by federal permit.

They have traps around their houses, generally wire cages or string nets. Bird banders get up early in the morning to see what birds their traps have captured; then they take these birds out carefully and put numbered aluminum bands on their legs, making a record of the number of the band, the species of bird, and the time and place it was banded. They then release the bird and send a card to the Federal Wildlife Service giving the number of the band and other information about the bird. If the bird bander captures a bird that has already been tagged, he makes a note of the number of the band, and sends this information to the Wildlife Service. This Service acts as a clearinghouse, informing bird banders of the wanderings of the birds they have tagged.

The purpose of this activity is to find out about the migration, dispersal, and other movements of birds. The data thus collected also give interesting information about the ages of birds, facts readily computed about dead birds from the dates when they were banded and their apparent ages then.

Chapter 13, "Bird Banding," discusses this activity in more detail.

Professional bird watchers

Occasionally you will meet a professional bird watcher. These are people who work for museums or make a living writing books about birds. A man I know who became a professional bird watcher is Dr. Josselyn Van Tyne. He was in my class at Harvard College, but I don't know whether he was interested in birds then, for we never went bird watching together. He has lately been president of the American Ornithologists' Union and is curator of birds at the University of Michigan. He makes interesting trips to the Arctic, Central America, and other areas to study birds' behavior. If you want to know anything about that rarest of American warblers, the Kirtland's, ask Dr. Van Tyne, because that is his specialty.

If you join the American Ornithologists' Union, chances are you will never become a full-fledged member. Most of those who achieve that distinction are professional bird watchers, members of museum staffs, who write learned pieces on subjects that are usually beyond the ken of the average bird watcher.

Related interests

It is hardly possible for a person with an active mind to be afield frequently in search of birds without developing other interests in natural history.

Many bird watchers are also interested in flowers; they associate the first Baltimore orioles with the first apple blossoms, the woodcock with the yellow flowers on the spicebush, and the late gentian with the southern flight of the geese.

Likewise, those afield in search of birds learn to know the trees —the white oaks, where the warblers feed, and the elms, where the orioles like to nest. They become acquainted with the various kinds of flies, crickets, and wasps. Sometimes they learn the rocks, and if they spend any time watching birds cross the moon, they may train their telescopes on other parts of the heavens and become familiar with some of the stars.

Although bird watchers seldom find any other phase of nature so fascinating as their own, still few of them lack at least a passing interest in these other aspects of the outdoors.

chapter 2 / Where to find birds

The bird watcher's chances of finding the objects of his quest are greatly improved if he knows what species to expect in the area or environment in which he happens to be. If you know that brown-headed nuthatches like the pine barrens of South Carolina, and happen to be in such an area, the chances are you will find the bird if you look hard enough. If you know that the European cormorant is the species found off New England in winter, the double-crested cormorant off the New Jersey coast, the Florida cormorant in the Southeast, and the olivaceous cormorant along the Gulf Coast, you are at least alerted for these possibilities.

Whenever I see a breakwater jutting into a bay or the ocean I expect, in winter, to find purple sandpipers. If there are piles farther out in the water, I look closely for cormorants sitting on top. In March I look for rusty blackbirds along little brooks, and

I never pass a stand of conifers that I do not search for long-eared owls. Sparrow hawks seem to like to perch on power lines along the road, and in the South they are joined by loggerhead shrikes, mourning doves, and meadowlarks. I never see a freshly plowed field that I do not expect killdeer, and whenever I find a rocky ridge in the woods I know that in season it may shelter worm-eating warblers. I am not generally disappointed when, in winter, I seek horned larks on airfields or other broad expanses. The winter my area was invaded by white-winged crossbills certainly demonstrated the fondness of these birds for hemlocks.

There are three general types of information the bird watcher needs in order to know where to find birds: (1) what birds live in various parts of the country; (2) what birds like special habitats, such as ocean beaches, bayberry thickets, open fields, fresh-water marshes, and so on; (3) what birds to look for at special spots, such as rocky jetties, haystacks, power lines, tops of small trees, piles, and other single places.

Pettingill's guides

The bird watcher's problem in respect to the first matter is readily solved. Olin Sewall Pettingill, Jr., has written two books that provide excellent specific information about what birds are found in various areas. They are *Bird Finding East of the Mississippi* (1951) and *Bird Finding West of the Mississippi* (1953). Dr. Pettingill takes the states one by one, and the areas of the states one by one, alphabetically, detailing what birds are to be expected in each place and explaining in detail how to reach such spots by motorcar or other conveyance.

Before exploring a new territory some distance from your home, even with the aid of Pettingill, it is well to try to make contact with friendly bird watchers there. If you inquire among your friends, you may discover someone who knows a bird watcher in the region you are to visit. If you are not successful, you might telephone the local bird club, museum, or even chamber of commerce. People who reside in areas strange to you can give information about where to look for birds and about the birds that are most likely to be encountered at the time of your visit.

Another way to capitalize on a visit to other areas is to go on a paid tour. The National Audubon Society conducts such tours in the Everglades National Park and Wildlife Refuge in Florida and in the Okeechobee-Kissimmee area.

Habitats preferred by birds

There are many places that Pettingill does not mention. A guide to bird finding in these spots is a knowledge of the preferences of birds for different habitats, as the tern for the ocean, the heron for the marsh, and the bluebird for the apple orchard. Let us look at the typical bird life of the following places, particularly as they exist in New Jersey, the area with which I am most familiar:

Ocean In the far ocean, shearwaters, petrels, jaegers, phalaropes; in the near ocean, gulls, terns, loons, and various species of ducks. Some of these birds of the near ocean are found at times on fresh-water lakes.

Beaches, dunes, thickets Sandpipers, plovers, horned larks; some sparrows, as song, Ipswich, and Savannah sparrows, and some hawks, as sparrow hawk, pigeon hawk, and osprey; herons, several warblers, catbird, red-winged blackbird, cedar waxwing.

Salt marshes and mud flats Egrets, herons, black-bellied plover, clapper rail, yellow-legs, Hudsonian curlew, long-billed marsh wren, swallows, sharp-tailed and seaside sparrows, short-eared owl.

Sounds, bays, and canals Canada goose, brant, and various species of ducks, including red-breasted merganser, scoters, and old-squaw; loons and grebes.

Lakes, rivers, and ponds Sixteen or more species of ducks, including American widgeon, black duck, teal, and pintail. Also coot, herons, and egrets. Semipalmated sandpiper, killdeer, black-bellied plover, pectoral sandpiper; tree, barn, and rough-winged swallows.

Fresh-water marshes Florida gallinule, Virginia and sora rails, American and least bittern, solitary sandpiper and Wilson's snipe, long-billed marsh wren; pintail, black duck, and blue-winged and green-winged teal; green heron and black-crowned night heron; swamp sparrow, marsh hawk.

Yards, orchards, and parks Most species of warblers; hairy and downy wood-peckers, chickadee, titmouse, and other feeding-station birds; song, white-throated, chipping, and tree sparrows; robin, bluebird, other thrushes; rose-breasted grosbeak, orioles, phoebe, pewee, chimney swift, nighthawk.

Fields Bobolink, meadowlark, pipit, horned lark, snow bunting. Various spar-rows, as field, song, vesper, and grasshopper sparrows. Cuckoo, thrasher, catbird, pheasant, flicker, grackle, goldfinch, and pine siskin; various warblers, as blue-winged warbler, parula warbler, Nashville warbler, prairie warbler, and redstart.

Higher trees Thrushes, vireos, crested flycatcher, various warblers; red-tailed, sharp-shinned, and Cooper's hawks; purple finch, kinglets, scarlet tanager.

Pine and oak barrens Towhee; chipping, field, and song sparrows; chickadee, blue jay, brown thrasher; sharp-shinned hawk; various warblers, as pine, black-and-white, parula, and myrtle warblers.

Mountain ridges Migrating hawks and eagles, especially the broad-winged, sharp-shinned, red-shouldered, red-tailed, Cooper's, pigeon, and duck hawks, and occasional ospreys and bald eagles. Hummingbirds, cedar waxwings, snow buntings, evening grosbeaks, and other species also seen migrating along the ridges.

Coniferous forests Long-eared owl, white-winged and red crossbills; pine siskin, pine grosbeak.

OCEAN. My experience with birds of the ocean has been along the eastern coast from Prince Edward Island to Georgia and along the Gulf of Mexico. I have set my telescope on the beach at Nauset on Cape Cod and seen dozens of Wilson's petrels far out on the ocean, flying over the waves like swallows. I have also seen the sooty shearwater in summer off the coast of Cape Cod. This was on the ocean side of Wellfleet; on the headlands there I set up my telescope and sighted the birds skimming on stiff wings two or three miles out at sea. The jaeger is an ocean bird, but I have seen parasitic jaegers off Cape May.

Winter, of course, is the time to look for the white-winged gulls. They are more likely to be found if a northeast wind is blowing. The Iceland, Kumlien's, and glaucous gulls are in this class. There are two rare gulls, natives of Europe, that you may also find in both winter and summer. They are the little and black-headed gulls. The best places I know for these birds are garbage dumps and sewage outlets along the coast.

I also see the cormorant offshore. Off the granite promontory of Cape Ann in Massachusetts I sight the European cormorant; off the Jersey shore the double-crested species stands motionless on the posts of fishing weirs or flies in long, fluid lines over the water. In March, off the coast of South Carolina, I have found the Florida cormorant, and in the same month, off the coast of Texas, the olivaceous variety.

BEACHES, DUNES, THICKETS. There is rich bird life along the ocean beaches and in the dunes that form their backbone. A typical area is Nauset Beach, which runs from Eastham on the lower arm of Cape Cod down to Chatham at the elbow. There you have the beach and behind the beach the sand dunes, and little else besides the beach grass and other low-growing plants. A somewhat similar area is Beach Haven Inlet off the Jersey shore, where there is a long stretch of beach backed by low dunes with very sparse vegetation. Farther north on the New Jersey shore is Island Beach, another fabulous barrier beach still in the primeval condition in which it existed for many thousands of years, because it has passed from a private estate to the State of New Jersey. On one side of this beach there is the ocean and on the other side Barnegat Bay; on the island itself are holly trees, poison ivy in profusion, and bayberry. These plants provide ample food for many species of birds. The great barrier beaches that stretch along the coast of Texas for 360 miles between Louisiana and Mexico are of similar formation, being long, slender islands or peninsulas that parallel the mainland and shelter intervening bays or lagoons.

SALT MARSHES AND MUD FLATS. One of the most fascinating experiences is to visit a heronry just half an hour before sunset. The heronry is likely to be situated in a clump of scrub oak and vines just off a salt marsh. You can watch black-crowned and yellow-crowned night herons stream out of their sanctuary to feed nocturnally in the marshes, and the other herons, the American and snowy egrets and the Louisiana, great blue, little blue, and green herons, come to roost.

One of the distinctive birds of the salt marshes is the clapper rail. Often you catch only a glimpse of its head sticking up through the grass and hear its distinctive "cha-cha-cha-cha-cha." The meadowlark is also distinctive of this habitat; I recall that in the Galveston area the Western meadowlark, which is the species found there, was almost the commonest bird, perching along the marshes on power lines and fence posts, and singing continually. The sharp-tailed sparrow likes both the coastal salt marshes and the inland prairie marshes.

For shore birds you can't beat the mud flats that often adjoin salt marshes. I think of the flats at the beginning of Nauset Beach on the bay side, not far from the house where Henry Beston lived the year that he wrote about in *Outermost House*. If you go there in the morning, so that the sun is behind your back, you can see curlews, plovers, sandpipers, in great number and variety.

SOUNDS, BAYS, AND CANALS. When I think of the bird life to be found in sheltered salt water, including bays, sounds, and canals, I recall the birds I have seen in Long Island Sound and in Massachusetts, Delaware, and New York Bays; in Cape Cod and Delaware and Chesapeake Canals, and other similar places. The ring-billed gull is common in Delaware Bay, and the great black-backed, herring, and laughing gulls are also found there. I remember the laughing gulls that followed the ferry that goes across part of Galveston Bay from Galveston Island to Bolivar Peninsula. A favorite pastime of ferry passengers is to toss pieces of bread high in the air and see the birds deftly catch them.

LAKES, RIVERS, AND PONDS. Included with lakes, rivers, and ponds should be reservoirs. These bodies of water provide sanctuaries for many species of waterfowl and shore birds. One of my favorite haunts is the Boonton Reservoir, source of Jersey City's water supply. This area is best in fall and winter, and I have seen sixteen or seventeen species of ducks there, including the American widgeon, scaup duck, ring-necked duck, American golden-eye, bufflehead, mallard, black duck, pintail, both varieties of teal, and American and hooded mergansers. Coots are numerous, and occasionally there is a flock of mute swans that have become feral, and, rarely, a whistling swan. You can also see Canada geese, herring gulls, pied-billed and horned grebes, and loons at this spot.

FRESH-WATER MARSHES. I am fortunate enough to live near two great fresh-water marshes, Troy Meadows and Hatfield Swamp. These areas are unusually rich in bird life, because they are combinations of actual marsh, dry islands, upland pastures, and groves of trees. The American and least bitterns are denizens of these areas, and you can hear the pumping noise of the former and see it if you paddle your canoe quietly along Troy Brook. I have come upon least bitterns standing motionless by the boardwalk that traverses the marsh. The Virginia and sora rails are also frequent here, and one of the characteristic sounds is the whinnying notes of the soras as they fly through the tall grasses. The black-crowned, green, and great blue herons are also found in this area, and a distinctive sound is the happy chatter of the long-billed marsh wren. The marsh is also the home of the Florida gallinule.

YARDS, ORCHARDS, AND PARKS. One of the best areas for bird watching is a park. I have wandered through many parks, and found the experience generally rewarding. I think of Central Park in Manhattan and Prospect Park in Brooklyn, Hermann and Memorial Parks in Houston, the Boston Garden and Common, and the many excellent parks of the Essex County park system in New Jersey. There are also various reservations that are parks in effect, such as Pound Ridge Reservation in Westchester County, New York, and the Watchung and South Mountain Reservations in New Jersey.

The range of bird life that you find in such areas is surprising. Some 225 species of birds have been found in New York City's Central Park, and I myself have seen the blue-gray gnatcatcher there and mallards nesting. I found the fulvous tree duck and the purple gallinule at a pond in Hermann Park in Houston, and little parks in my own neighborhood have provided wood ducks, redheads, white-winged crossbills, evening grosbeaks, and many other species. A man I know goes to work in Manhattan two hours early each day in order to watch the birds in City Hall and Battery Parks and in St. Paul's and Trinity Churchyards. He and two fellow bird watchers have counted 115 species at these places.

FIELDS. An important aspect of the general habitat of fields is the airport. I go to nearby airports to find the horned larks in late November and late February. In early December I have found snow buntings there and an occasional Lapland longspur with them. Moreover, it was at an airport near Newburyport, Massachusetts, that I saw my first upland sandpipers.

HIGHER TREES. Besides various sparrows and woodpeckers, there are many warblers to be found in the tall trees. It is especially inspiring to look at the high crowns of the oaks in spring as the tender green leaves are just beginning to appear. These are what I call warbler trees, because there I find the Blackburnian, bay-breasted, magnolia, Cape May, chestnut-sided, and many other gaily colored warblers. One of the most exciting experiences in bird watching is the pursuit of warblers in the spring; and the tops of the trees are generally the best places to find them.

PINE AND OAK BARRENS. In my state there are vast areas characterized chiefly by their sand and pines. There are similar areas on Cape Cod, and I have also gone birding around Fort Bragg in North Carolina, where sand and longleaf pine and various varieties of scrub oak are dominant.

The red-eyed towhee is a typical bird of the New Jersey pine barrens, as the area is called, and chipping, field, and song sparrows are common. Chickadees are frequent in the Cape Cod area, and also hermit thrushes, thrashers, and blue jays. In the Southern pinelands I have found the brown-headed nuthatch and red-bellied woodpecker; and other woodpeckers, nuthatches, and brown creepers are abundant in these areas. The pine warbler prefers the barrens in South Carolina, Georgia, and New Jersey, I have found and the black-and-white and parula warblers are also found there.

MOUNTAIN RIDGES. My bird watching along mountain ridges has taken place in New Jersey, along both the Watchung and Kittatinny Mountain ridges, and also at Hawk Mountain in Pennsylvania, which is in the Blue Ridge Mountains. Hawks and eagles coast along the ridges on the updrafts, and in the fall you see broad-winged hawks go by in hundreds, sometimes in swirling "kettles" of birds. The other species are less numerous as to individuals, although in one day an observer may count from one to two thousand hawks of several species passing overhead. At Hawk Mountain, where Maurice Broun has protected the hawks from hunters in the sanctuary established by Mrs. Rosalie Edge, golden eagles and gyrfalcons have also been recorded.

CONIFEROUS FORESTS. Long-eared owls have a pronounced liking for stands of evergreens, and betray their presence by dropping pellets that contain the remains of birds and mice that they have devoured. Traces of their droppings on the tree bark is also evidence of the birds' presence. It was in the coniferous forests of Nova Scotia that I first saw white-winged crossbills, and when these northern finches invaded New Jersey in the winter of 1952–53, they invariably sought stands of hemlocks. Red crossbills also frequent evergreen woods. I first saw this species in a pine near the shore of the Ottawa River in Canada.

OTHER HABITATS. There are other habitats, distinctive of other parts of the country, that have their own bird life. Tundras, plains and prairies, deserts, and canyons are among such habitats, and there are many others.

Preferences for perches

Many birds possess almost characteristic preferences for particular places or positions. The liking of sparrow hawks for power lines, of goldfinches for thistles, of crossbills for hemlocks, are so ingrained as to amount to characteristics. This subject will be discussed in Chapter 3, "How to Approach and Identify Birds."

chapter 3/ How to approach and identify birds

In going afield to watch birds, the beginner has first the problem of getting near enough to the creatures so that he can see them properly, and then the problem of identifying them.

How to approach birds

The subject of how to approach birds is concerned with how to walk, the kinds of clothing to wear and equipment to use, and the matters of light, weather, and other considerations.

CAUTIOUS MOVEMENTS. Birds have excellent eyesight and hearing, and are easily startled. This is especially true of some of the larger birds, such as hawks. So the bird watcher should approach birds cautiously. He should wear clothing of subdued color that blends with the background. He should not swing his arms; I often hold my hands behind my back when I am trying to move quite close to a bird. When I was a boy bird watcher, I stalked birds successfully by creeping on hands and knees. There is less inclination to do this as you advance in years. However, it is well to take advantage of cover, moving behind trees and other natural objects in order to gain concealment. It is better to use a zig-zag approach than to walk directly toward a bird. Movements should sometimes be so slow as to be almost imperceptible to the bird; raise glasses slowly and refrain from pointing quickly. Avoid walking heavily or stepping on twigs that crack. Loud talking should also be shunned, although some birds have their hearing pitched so high that ordinary conversation does not bother them. Warblers are such birds.

RECLINING OR SITTING POSITION. Birds have somehow gotten to beware of men and women who walk or stand, but they are not so cautious about those in other positions. I am impressed with how readily the birds take me for granted in the summer when I lie in my hammock in the yard. Apparently the recumbent form is not so fearsome as the perpendicular.

Another excellent way to observe birds is to choose a suitable spot and sit down. You will find that birds do not shun the quiet, sitting figure. After a while all manner of feathered creatures will appear, birds that you would not have suspected were in the neighborhood had you merely walked through. There are two times of year when this practice is not satisfactory: one is the dead of summer when there is little movement among the birds; the other is the depth of winter. You must keep moving if you want to see birds at these times.

USE OF CONVEYANCES. Birds seem relatively unafraid of auto-mobiles, and sometimes they may be approached on horseback better than on foot. Some of the most satisfactory birding I have experienced has been by rowboat and canoe. I have rowed quietly along the shore of many a lake, surprising the kingbirds, king-fishers, and herons along the edge, or watching the ospreys and vultures soar overhead. I have also glided along streams that were remote from people and motorcars, finding red-headed and pileated woodpeckers in the trees along the watercourse, killdeer, herons, and ducks in the marshy edges of the river, and warblers everywhere. Birds seem to regard a canoe as casually as they would a log floating downstream. Also, it is possible by canoeing to reach more remote regions that may hold surprises in the bird life they offer.

SUN AT YOUR BACK. If possible, have the sun at your back and shining full on the bird. However, avoid letting the light strike bright metallic objects or glass, as the reflection might startle your subject. It is sometimes desirable to plan a whole field trip so that the sun is at your back. If you approach certain areas at the wrong time of day you will be unable to see the birds because you will be looking into the sun. I like Nauset Beach on Cape Cod in the morning, for instance, as in the afternoon you have to look into the sun on the bay side where the shore birds are, and all you discern are silhouettes that are interesting but rather hard to identify. In bird watching along the Jersey shore we find it advantageous to go directly south early in the morning and then work back, rather than work south, as the light is more favorable the first way.

TIME OF DAY TO GO AFIELD. The best time of day for bird observation is early morning or late afternoon. More birds can be seen before seven o'clock of a spring morning than during all the rest of the day. They are awakening and feeding then, and are most active. This is especially true of birds that have just arrived after a long step in their migratory flight. In fact, it is well to go afield very early on mornings in the spring, because you can identify many birds, such as the owls and marsh birds, by their calls before it is light enough to see them, and then with sunrise there is a perfect torrent of song. Birds feed in the late afternoon before retiring for the night, so that is another good time to observe them. Early morning and late afternoon are ordinarily times when there is little wind, and this helps in observation. When the day is still, you can see any movement in the trees, but in a brisk breeze the leaves are so agitated that bird movements are concealed.

Moreover, I have found that birds generally do not like wind and seek protected spots.

WHAT ABOUT SEASONS? Although there is nothing like a crisp May morning for bird watching, other seasons are also profitable. In July many young birds are about. Some of the migratory birds begin to drift down along the beaches from the north, and others that have reared their young in our areas begin to slip away to the south. I find that all seasons of the year are fascinating where I live, the month that has the least movement among the birds being January. By the middle of February some of the birds that have wintered farther south and pass through on their way to the far north come back, such as the northern horned larks, snow buntings, and Lapland longspurs; and the same month sees the arrival of pintails, robins, red-winged blackbirds, fox sparrows, and a long list of other birds.

September is magnificent for the great southward passage of the flocks, for the hawk flights along the mountain ridges, and for watching birds pass the face of the full moon. There is continual southern movement of the birds until Christmas, with species from the north drifting down and those that normally pass the winter to the south of us lingering for some weeks, but finally departing. The Christmas counts prove a kind of climax of activity for the bird year, producing last year 92 species of birds in the area in which I live, that is, a circle of 15 miles diameter, while bird watchers who went to the beaches just to the south of us compiled a list of 117 species. Fifteen bird clubs that in 1953 took a Christmas census in New Jersey tallied 171 species and 391,671 individuals.

WHAT ABOUT WEATHER? Should you stay indoors on bad days? Not a bit of it. The members of one of the bird clubs in my neighborhood say that they have observed over the last twenty-one years that it makes no difference what the weather is at the time of their Christmas censuses as far as the success of their listing is concerned. The day when they compiled the largest list afforded the foulest weather. Birds, except waterfowl and shore birds, seem to seek shelter to a certain extent during heavy rains, but they are active during warm, light showers. Someone has said that if you want to see unusual birds, go out in the teeth of a gale. This is true along our ocean shore if the wind is blowing from the east or northeast, as it blows in the alcids, such as guillemots, puffins, and razor-billed auks. After one storm in Massachusetts there were some twenty thousand dovekies seen along the shore. A strong wind off the ocean is also likely to bring the little and black-headed gulls—European species that wander only irregularly to our shores.

In my region, some of the best birding is done with a strong northwest wind following a drop in temperature. That seems to send the hawks spiraling southward in the fall. They drift down the mountain ridges, churning along in great "kettles" of birds that may bring two thousand hawks of assorted species winging overhead in one day in one spot. Such winds in the fall also tend to blow other migrating birds out to sea, and in New Jersey they hug the coast, becoming concentrated in the southern extremity of the state, at Cape May Point. There, on good days in September and October, it is possible to see unbelievable concentrations of birds of 150 or so different species.

Clothing and equipment

Proper clothing and correct equipment will also add to the success of the bird watcher.

WHAT CLOTHING TO WEAR. I make good use of old Army clothing, finding that khaki slacks and shirt in the summer are the right color, harmonizing well enough with most backgrounds, especially those along sandy shores. In the summer I wear sneakers or tennis shoes when walking on the sands, as I find these most comfortable, and if they get wet they dry quickly. For walking in the woods and fields I find a leather shoe of the Army type to be most suitable. It is well to have good headgear, and in summer I find that a khaki cap with a visor is most desirable, as the visor protects the eyes from the sun and the shape of the cap prevents its blowing off in the wind.

In winter it is also desirable to be dressed in clothing that has a khaki or greenish color. On cool days of spring and fall I wear my olive-drab Army field jacket, but in winter more special clothing is necessary. Bird watching in this season can be a very cold occupation, because it is done in exposed areas and does not usually entail violent exercise that may warm the participant, as does skiing or skating. Bird watching along ocean beaches in the winter is especially cold; I have stood on rocky promontories along the ocean in winter, with a sharp wind blowing, and found that even the warmest clothing was barely adequate. Boat trips in winter in search of birds of the open sea are also cold operations, as they are often taken in open craft. I wear a cap with ear flaps and a long coat with khaki on the outside and a lining of sheepskin and alpaca. This has a waterproof mouton collar that may be pulled up almost to the eyes. My wife, who is my constant companion in bird watching, wears a similar coat, but of a maroon color. Some women's coats have hoods of fur or other warm material. I also wear heavy fleece-lined gloves (also Army issue) in the winter, and heavy wool trousers.

Far be it from me to prescribe clothing for women bird watchers. However, my wife wears slacks both summer and winter. She wears the same type of cap that I do, with sun visor. In winter it is made of heavy material and has ear flaps.

The best footgear in winter is a high boot with rubber soles that will cover a heavy wool sock. These boots may be purchased in sporting-goods stores. There is nothing more miserable than being cold and wet while bird-watching in winter, and protective clothing cannot be overemphasized.

It is well to have a pair of sunglasses stuck in a pocket for use in both summer and winter.

INSECT REPELLENT. The bird watcher may get into insect-infested areas in the summer, so it is well to be equipped with insect repellent. Many beaches are notoriously uncomfortable because of biting flies, mosquitoes, and gnats. Inland you find mosquitoes, black flies, and ticks. I have looked for birds in some areas that were so mosquito-infested, as the Hackensack Meadows in New Jersey, that I have spread mosquito netting over my hat and tucked it in my coat, to protect my face, and have worn cotton gloves to protect my hands.

BINOCULARS. The serious bird watcher needs a pair of binoculars. The most popular size is the 7 x 35 binocular, which affords an image seven times as large as that seen with the unaided eye. For details about the different sizes of binoculars and their care see Chapter 8, "What about Glasses?"

BOOKS. The bird watcher will want to take afield a guide to help him identify the species he sees. The guide I use is Roger Tory Peterson's *A Field Guide to the Birds*. For information about other field guides and reference books see Chapter 9, "Books about Birds."

NOTEBOOK, CHECK LIST. It is desirable when afield to make a record of the birds you see and interesting happenings. Details of the kinds of notebook, check list, and other records that may be useful are found in Chapter 10, "Should You Keep Records?"

How to identify birds

There are eight main clues to the identification of birds: their color, size, song, flight, walk, posture, shape, and the habitats in which they are found.

IDENTIFYING BIRDS BY THEIR FLIGHT. Manner of flight of birds should be studied by the bird watcher, for it is a principal means of identifying them. The goldfinch can be told by its bounding flight as it flies over a field, singing its gay "per-chic-o-ree" as it goes. The woodpeckers also have an undulating flight, as they rise with a few wing beats and slide downward with the wings partly closed. If you see a bird fly in this manner and then alight on the trunk of a tree rather than perch on a branch, you can be sure it is a woodpecker.

Turkey vultures are distinguished by their graceful, soaring flight; they glide in wide circles, hardly ever seeming to flap their wings. The bird student who lives in an area where both the turkey and black vultures are found knows that the latter has a more labored flight.

Some hawks also are readily distinguished by their flight. A large gray or brown bird, flying slowly near the ground, alternat-

ing a few beats of its long wings with glides, is apt to be a marsh
hawk. It has a white rump and sails with wings held, not flat, but
at an angle over its back; this distinguishes it positively from the
rough-legged hawk, which may be found in the same habitat. A
small hawk that hovers on rapidly beating wings in one spot is
a sparrow hawk. The sharp-shinned hawk, of similar size, flies
with several quick wing beats and a sail.

If you see a bird (often a pair) larger than a robin fly up from
the ground and note a long pointed tail bordered with white and
hear a whistling sound, it is a mourning dove. The whistling sound
is caused by the air passing through its wings.

Most other birds have distinctive flights, and as the bird watcher
gains in experience he will become familiar with them and use
them for quick identification.

IDENTIFICATION BY WALK. The movement of birds other than
by flight is also a means of identification. If you see a bird wagging
its tail up and down while walking, you can suppose it to be a
pipit, a water thrush, an oven-bird, or a palm warbler, because
this habit is ingrained in these species. If you see a bird going
down a tree headfirst, you know it is a nuthatch. This tree climber
does not use its stubby tail to brace itself against the tree trunks
in climbing, as do the woodpeckers. Cowbirds can easily be distinguished from other blackbirds with which they may be feeding
by their smaller size and their habit of lifting their tails high as
they walk.

A black-and-white bird that is smaller than a sparrow and
creeps along trunks and branches is surely a black-and-white
warbler, and none of the other warblers have this form of locomo-
tion. Birds that you see swimming low in the water, sometimes
with only head or neck showing, are likely to be loons or grebes.
The pied-billed grebe has the faculty of gradually submerging
itself in the water until it disappears entirely.

The motions of birds in feeding are also identifying characteristics. A foot-long shore bird found on open beaches that feeds
like a sewing machine, rapidly jabbing its long bill into the mud,
is a dowitcher. This characteristic has earned it the local name
of "sewing-machine bird." If you also see on the shore a group
of small, plump sandpipers that chase the retreating waves and

then in turn retreat before them, there is the good chance that you see sanderlings. A small sandpiper that is found along lakes and streams throughout the country and that teeters up and down as it walks is the spotted sandpiper. The solitary sandpiper often teeters, but not so pronouncedly as the spotted.

IDENTIFICATION BY POSTURE. Some birds have such distinctive postures when standing or perching as readily to identify them. In March you may see a gray-and-white bird, a little larger than a house sparrow, perched on a low tree. If it wags its tail persistently, chances are it is a phoebe, for tail wagging is a characteristic of this flycatcher. A somewhat similar trait is displayed by the sparrow hawk. It sits fairly erect, often on a power line, but gives an occasional jerk of its tail. A large, dark sandpiper that is found on the edges of ponds and streams may often be seen standing still and solemnly nodding its head. This nodding habit is a field mark of the solitary sandpiper.

A big brown marsh bird that stands with its bill pointed skyward is the American bittern, while a black-and-white duck with rufous-red sides that sits on the water with its large, spatulate bill pointing downward is the shoveller. If you see a very tall bird standing motionless on the edge of a pool or stream, chances are it is a great blue heron or an American egret. Or you may be walking along the ocean and see piles or poles of fishing weirs offshore, with a dark bird sitting on each. If they are perched in an upright position, rather than somewhat horizontally as gulls stand, you have cormorants in view.

IDENTIFICATION BY COLOR. Color is probably the easiest clue to the identification of birds. Sometimes it is the only feature observed. The bird watcher in tracking down a new bird should take written notes while he is looking at the bird or immediately afterward, because it is amazing how soon memory can become confused on these points. Write down the color of the sides and top of head, back and sides of neck, back, wings, and tail; next put down the color of underparts, throat, front of neck, breast, and belly. Note any conspicuous mark or color. The red shoulder of the red-winged blackbird is distinctive, as is the black V on the yellow breast of the meadowlark. The yellow feet or so-called "golden slippers" of the snowy egret distinguish it from other herons, and the red tail of the red-tailed hawk is a sure field mark. If the bird is small and greenish it may be a vireo, and in such case it is well to note whether the bird has white wing bars or not, for in the East three of the vireos lack such bars, while three other species possess them.

IDENTIFICATION BY SIZE. Size of the bird is most important. Here it is well to have a rough guide, to the effect that a house sparrow is approximately 6 inches long, a robin is 10, and a crow approximately 20. There is much variation even in the sizes of these three birds, as Eastern crows run from 17 to 21 inches in length, for instance. It will help, however, if the bird watcher can tell whether the species he sees is approximately larger or smaller than these three common birds.

It is well to have a list available, or have some idea in your own mind, of the relative sizes of various birds of the same general groups or families. Pough includes such lists in his *Audubon Water Bird Guide*. One of them is called "Comparative Average Lengths of Waders," and it lists the species in order of size from the black rail, which has an overall length of 5½ inches, to the limpkin, which stretches 26. If you are looking at sandpipers and see one that is slightly larger than the sanderling with which you are familiar, you will then suspect that it is more likely to be the stilt sandpiper at 8½ inches than the Western sandpiper at 6½.

IDENTIFICATION BY SONG. Familiarity with bird notes is not only a great source of pleasure, but also a major aid to the quick identification of birds. If you are walking through the woods in spring and hear a sharp metallic "kick" or "eek," you know that a rose-breasted grosbeak is in the trees nearby, without having to hear the pure, mellow, and beautiful warble of the bird or to see its rose-red breast and striking black-and-white coloration. Or if you are sitting in your house and hear a short, thin "chip" outside, you know immediately that a cardinal has come to feed. Call notes and songs of birds are, with colors, the readiest means of identification. There are four ways to become familiar with bird songs. One is to associate the song with the bird that you have identified in other ways, as by its color, shape, or size. Then, when you are afield, you can identify the bird by hearing its song, even if you cannot see the singer. Another way is to look up the description of the song in one of the field guides; you will first be obliged, however, to possess some general notion of the kind of bird you are looking for. In other words, if you hear two crows, and one sounds as if it had a cold, you can look in your field guide and find that the rough voice is distinctive of the fish crow. Remember, however, that young American crows in their first summers sound like fish crows. In the same way, if you hear a warbler whose notes are a husky "zur, zur, zree," you may look through the descriptions of these species' songs and find that this one belongs to the black-throated blue warbler. Then try to identify this bird by its colors, and listen again for it to sing. In this way you will associate the bird and its voice.

A third way to identify birds by their songs is to use a good book on birds' songs, such as Aretas A. Saunders' *A Guide to Bird Songs*. This author has developed an ingenious method of diagraming birds' songs that helps in their identification. A fourth and one of the best methods is to listen to records. I remember one summer when I was at Cape Cod and heard a bird song that I was never able to associate with a bird that I saw, other than to get a fleeting glimpse of a smallish brown form. Then I came home and put on Jerry Stillwell's first long-playing record of forty-seven bird songs, and heard the song I had listened to on the Cape, identifying it immediately and unmistakably as the Carolina wren. I had searched for a description of the song in field guides, but had found none that exactly tallied. The most complete set of bird records is that called "American Bird Songs," recorded by Albert R. Brand and obtainable from the Comstock Publishing Company in Ithaca, New York. It includes six double-disk records.

Songbirds of America in Color, Sound, and Story, by ARTHUR A. ALLEN and PETER P. KELLOGG, was developed and published in cooperation with Cornell University Press by Book-Records, Inc., New York. This so-called "soundbook" includes 24 natural-color photographs by Dr. Allen, high-fidelity recording of 24 familiar song birds supervised by Dr. Kellogg, and text and commentary keyed to the photographs and recording.

Bird Songs of Dooryard, Field, and Forest, Vols. 1 and 2, Ficker

Recording Service, Old Greenwich, Connecticut, covers 275 songs and calls of 96 different North American bird species.

In the region in which I live there may be found close to forty different species of warblers, ranging in color from the bright orange of the Blackburnian to the dull olive of the worm-eating warbler. Obviously, the distinctive notes of some of these species are definite helps in sorting them out from their fellows. This is especially true in the case of birds whose songs are unmistakable and of shy birds, more often heard than seen. The Kentucky warbler is a case in point. I once spent a full forenoon listening to the song of this species but was never able to see it, although I tried hard to track it down in the dense foliage of June.

It is possible to produce birdlike noises with a bird call or bird squeaker. These have become quite popular in the United States since the war, but they have been used in Europe for many years. The squeaky sounds produced by these devices may attract catbirds, white-eyed vireos, chickadees, and other species. However, it requires two hands to operate a bird call, so some bird watchers prefer to make kissing sounds with the mouth against the back of one hand while the other hand holds the binoculars.

IDENTIFICATION BY SHAPE. Whether a bird is slim or stout, whether it has a thin or a heavy bill, is important in identification. Roger Tory Peterson's field guides emphasize birds' roadside and flight silhouettes. In connection with hawks, for instance, you will learn that the buteos or buzzard hawks are chunky with broad wings and broad, rounded tails. Such hawks include the red-tailed, red-shouldered, and broad-winged hawks, to mention three of the commonest. The accipiters, on the other hand, have short, rounded wings and long tails. They include the sharp-shinned and Cooper's hawks; the falcons, including the sparrow and duck hawks, have long, pointed wings and long tails.

If you see a small bird with an upturned tail it is in all probability a wren. You can refine your identification by considering that if you see it in the winter it may be a winter wren; if you see it about your house it may be a house wren or a Carolina wren, and if you see it in a marsh it will be the short-billed or long-billed marsh wren, the former commonly frequenting grassy and the latter cattail marshes.

A great deal can be told by the bird's beak. Small birds with stubby, heavy beaks are likely to be seed eaters, like sparrows or finches; those with thin, fine beaks are more likely to be warblers or vireos or other insect-eating birds. The brown creeper has a fine beak, ideal for picking grubs out of the bark of trees. If you see a bird whose bill is actually crossed, chances are it is a white-winged or a red crossbill, and a long-billed curlew once seen can never be forgotten, because its down-curved bill is fully six inches long. I knew immediately the first long-billed curlew I saw, because it fitted so exactly the descriptions I had read.

IDENTIFICATION BY HABITAT. One of the best clues to the identity of a bird is the environment in which it is found. This subject is discussed in detail in Chapter 2, "Where to Find Birds." If you find a wren in a cattail marsh, the chances are it is a long-billed marsh wren rather than a short-billed species, for the latter prefers wet meadows and grassy marshes. You are likely to find the American merganser on creeks, rivers, and lakes, whereas the red-breasted merganser prefers the ocean. Similarly, among the swallows you find the tree swallows in open wooded swamps, the rough-winged species breeding in banks or masonry, the barn swallow about barns and buildings. These associations are invaluable to the bird watcher in his identifications, and they must be gained from observation and study.

chapter 4 / What to feed birds

Why feed birds? Because it's fun for bird watchers and good for the birds. I recall one year when we found particular enjoyment in scarlet tanagers. A cold, wet spring had retarded the development of cankerworms, and returning tanagers seemed especially affected by the absence of these accustomed morsels. In lieu of worms, the birds eagerly attacked suet provided for them, and they visited our feeding stations repeatedly. They were aggressive and fought off other species, but one day we saw a tanager, a Baltimore oriole, and a blue jay feeding together on a single window tray. So many bright feathers right at our kitchen window made an experience long to be remembered.

RARITIES ATTRACTED. Another pleasure is the chance of attracting rarities. There was a memorable invasion of evening grosbeaks in the winter of 1949–50, and nearly everyone in our area who kept a feeding station reported these rare visitors from the north. An acquaintance in a nearby town seems to have a certain magic with these big finches, and I have seen half a hundred at her place in years when no one else in the region could boast a single bird. She keeps grosbeaks so late that in May I have seen evening and rose-breasted grosbeaks feeding there at the same time. Then there was the morning we discovered pine grosbeaks eating seed we had scattered on a spot in our driveway that had been cleared of snow. There had been no reports of pine grosbeaks elsewhere in our area that winter, so the birds' visit was an exciting surprise.

Some of the most interesting bird records are contributed by people who are not expert bird watchers and who seldom if ever go on field trips. But they do feed birds, and rarities have a habit of dropping down on the humblest feeding stations. One woman who lives in a North Jersey mining town noticed one day that a strange, yellowish-green bird was feeding in the company of sparrows and starlings outside her living-room window. She studied her bird books and decided it was a Western tanager, although the bird had been recorded only once previously in the whole region around New York City. The tanager remained all winter, so for the next several weeks the woman was besieged by visitors who wanted to see her rare find and add a new bird to their life lists. The day I saw the bird I also signed the lady's guest register, and found there close to two hundred names of bird watchers from four states and the District of Columbia. This same winter, dickcissels, previously rare in New Jersey, kept bobbing up among the drab sparrows feeding at modest window trays, and one woman in Boonton discovered to her own and everyone's amazement that she was hostess to a Bullock's oriole, a species never before recorded in the Garden State.

DAY-TO-DAY VISITORS. The day-to-day pleasure is the company of the chickadees and titmice, the nuthatches and downy woodpeckers, the jays and juncos, and other birds that seem to make your yard their home. The feeding-station operator comes to know the personalities of species and individuals, the times they prefer to feed, the many variations in their calls and songs.

PLEASURE FOR SHUT-INS. Those who are ill or confined indoors for other reasons derive a very special kind of pleasure from feeding birds. I do not believe I ever appreciated the birds around my house so keenly as one winter when I was recovering from a long spell of pneumonia. My bedroom window overlooked the feeding stations, so I could watch the cautious arrival of the cardinal, the blustering deportment of the jay, and the industry of the hairy woodpecker that was a frequent visitor that year. A friend of mine was never particularly interested in birds until his recuperation from a coronary attack. Then he began to photograph them from his window, and I am sure his recovery was hastened by pleasure over daily visits from a saw-whet owl.

BIRDS EAT INSECTS. Bird watchers who are also gardeners will benefit from the birds' work in destroying insects.

Benefits for birds

Feeding is good for the birds. It will be easy to see how the bird population in your neighborhood increases as the birds are given food and shelter. The Fish and Wildlife Service estimates that there are on the average only 2 birds to an acre, but that this figure has been increased to 59 in the most successful programs of protection and encouragement.

HELP IN BAD WEATHER. Of course, birds are in especial need of help in times of storm and drought. When deep snow or heavy ice covers birds' natural food, the feeding-station operator should be especially liberal and regular in his offerings. I have noticed that birds seem to sense an approaching snowstorm and feed avidly both before and during the storm.

Severe storms sometimes require that bird watchers, sportsmen, and government agencies rally to the birds' aid. In January, 1948, for instance, after the great snow that had blanketed the East late the previous month, paper bags of seed were dropped from airplanes over wild areas otherwise hardly accessible. One year the

National Audubon Society, alarmed at the plight of birds whose food was buried under deep snow, got the Post Office to co-operate in a relief program. The latter announced that bird lovers might mail cracked corn and small grain, to be scattered by rural mail carriers along their routes. Sufficient address was "Mr. and Mrs. Bird, R.F.D."

Drought also has its hardships for birds. In the summer of 1949, for instance, destruction of vegetation and insects by the pro-longed dry spell made it hard for birds to get enough food. Lack of rain hardened the soil, and robins looked in vain for worms, which had retreated deep beneath the ironbound lawns. Drought may be especially hard on recently fledged birds left to fend for themselves. Lacking experience, they do not know enough to leave higher nesting areas for the lower, moister meadows. Bird watchers should keep water in their bird baths and supply scraps from their tables and other food. If they go away on vacations they might engage a neighbor's boy to maintain such services to the birds.

I put out a small amount of food all summer, for while the birds do not need it unless there is a drought, it does keep more of them in my neighborhood.

Cautions on feeding programs

Anyone who begins a feeding program should feel that it is his responsibility to continue it. A supply of food and water sub-stantially in excess of what an area naturally affords will support a larger bird population, but the birds will be in sore straits if this sustenance is suddenly taken away. If feeding of birds is begun early in the fall, for instance, so that individuals which normally migrate south are induced to linger around feeding stations, then the birds face tragedy if the feeding is discontinued. They are not used to foraging for themselves in northern latitudes in the winter, and it will then be too late for them to build up the heavy layers of fat that enable migrating birds to travel long distances with a minimum of food along the way. Some bird watchers un-thinkingly suggest that feeding should be started early in the fall for the sake of holding some birds that normally pass to the south.

This seems to me to be a selfish practice, exposing the birds to unnecessary hazards for the pleasure of the bird watcher.

POSSIBLE HAZARDS FOR BIRDS. Some ornithologists question whether there is actually a net gain for birds in feeding-station operations. They reason that the artificial protection and encouragement given birds tends to promote the propagation of weaker species and to prolong the lives of sick or feeble birds that would otherwise fail in the struggle for survival. They also feel that unless feeding stations are kept clean, they tend to spread disease because of the unnatural congregations of birds that they attract. Coccidiosis, for instance, is a deadly disease found among both wild and domestic fowl, and it is spread by droppings. A feeding station that is not kept clean is therefore an agency for the spread of this disease. The periodic fluctuations in the populations of some species of birds are attributed to disease. A study of English grouse revealed, for instance, that when the birds became very numerous the ground upon which they congregated became infected. This facilitated the spread of disease among them and reduced their number. It is obvious that the abnormally large populations of birds at feeding stations may similarly be conducive to the spreading of disease. The best preventive is cleanliness.

Natural food of birds

This chapter is concerned with the food that is supplied birds on feeding stations, suet sticks, and other devices, and not with the natural food provided by plantings. In their natural state, winter birds eat berries, leftover grain, fruit, weed and grass seeds, and insects. Accordingly, birds that explore decayed wood and the bark of trees for grubs will gladly accept suet as a substitute, and vegetarians will take proffered grain.

They like food in familiar forms, but will accept some innovations. Birds select their food in various ways, using experience, sight, and touch. The Japanese beetle looks different from the beetles our native birds feed upon; hence they have been slow to accept it as an item of diet, only the adaptable starling being very progressive in that respect. Arthur A. Allen writes that for twenty-five years he had a persimmon tree in his yard in New York State, but never saw a bird take the fruit, whereas there are 16 species of birds that feed upon it in the South. It is well known that hummingbirds prefer red, notably in cardinal flowers, salvia, and bergamot. However, one bird watcher experimented with sunflower seed and purple finches. When she painted the seed bright red the birds would not touch it, although it was left out for a month. When she dyed the seed blue the birds accepted it after a few days. Rodent exterminators have found that birds will not touch poisoned grain that has been colored, because the sight of it is unfamiliar. Rats and mice will take it because they find their food to a great extent by smell.

Among winter birds, red cedar and juniper berries rank high for food, and bayberry, dogwood, elderberry, and sumac are accepted by an even greater number. Raspberry and blackberry are unrivaled in popularity in season, but the season is short. Blueberry is also held in high esteem. Wild grapes, wild roses, privet, bittersweet, and barberry are eaten by many species. The long-lasting fruits of barberry tide birds over bitter winter days. I have seen overwintering orioles, lacking wild grapes, fare well on the thick-fleshed grapes bought during the cold months in markets and provided by sympathetic bird watchers.

FOOD ELEMENTS. Ordinarily birds procure proper food elements in their daily diets. Sumac fruits are high in vitamin A, important for the vitality of certain cell tissues, but low in other elements; hence they are taken by the birds only after other foods are depleted. A study of stomachs of flickers that had starved one winter in Iowa showed that they were much weakened by improper food. Unable to find the ants and other insects that ordinarily constitute half their food supply, they had fed too largely upon sumac and other indigestible seeds. Birds also find vitamin A in various fruits and berries, rose hips, smartweed seeds, bittersweet, and yellow corn. Quails with a good storage of vitamin A have been put on a diet high in every nutritive element except vitamin A. Within a few weeks they exhausted their stored supply and died.

Protein comes from sunflower seed, peanut butter, hemp seed. Salt is provided in peanut butter and bread; birds do not usually

take free salt, but will eat salty substances. However, pine grosbeaks have been seen feeding on the salt emptied from an ice
cream freezer. Calcium and phosphorus are found in grit. Carbo-
hydrates are provided in corn, millet, and wheat. Fats are found in
suet, peanut butter, and pecan and other nut meats.

What food to provide

It is desirable to look at a bird-feeding program somewhat from
the point of view of the birds. It is not reasonable to assume that
all birds everywhere find the same birdseed mixture equally acceptable. Reasonably careful observation will reveal which foods
the birds like best and which they disregard completely. It is
possible for anyone to conduct a test such as that done by the
Audubon Nature Center at Greenwich, Connecticut. Measured
amounts of nine different seeds were placed in as many containers,
and a record kept of the speed with which each variety was eaten.
First choice of seed-eating birds was sunflower, with small millets
next in preference. Peanuts, milo, whole corn, and oats were eaten
in approximately equal quantities, but buckwheat, wheat, hemp,
rice, and cracked corn were almost disregarded. It depends upon
your birds, because cracked corn is known to be eaten by jays,
grackles, mourning doves, and tree sparrows.

SUET. Suet is one of the most economical and best-accepted bird
foods. I now get it without charge from my butcher, although
there was a time right after the war when it cost twenty cents a
pound.

Suet is eaten by chickadees, downy and hairy woodpeckers,
flickers, nuthatches, tufted titmice, brown creepers, golden- and
ruby-crowned kinglets, blue jays, and starlings. It is also taken
eagerly by insectivorous birds that arrive from the south early
in spring, sometimes before their normal diet of insects is ready.

Don't be stingy with suet, but put out a piece as big as your
fist. Tie it to a tree with several windings of white cotton string
for an easy and effective method of dispensing. Some women
crochet suet holders, small bags with large interstices. I sometimes use the loosely woven bags that oranges come in, first soak-
ing the bag in a bleaching agent to rid it of its bright reddish color.

Other types of suet holders will be discussed in Chapter 5, "Bird Baths and Feeders."

In the same classification of food as suet are table fats that may be melted and poured into holes in a stick or otherwise dispensed. Pieces of cooked meat may be put out, and bones that retain shreds of meat may be hung from trees.

SEEDS. Sunflower seed is most popular with birds; it is also most expensive, running around twenty-five cents a pound in amounts up to ten pounds in my town. You will want a generous amount of sunflower in your seed ration if you have chickadees, evening grosbeaks, pine grosbeaks, cardinals, blue jays, woodpeckers, nuthatches, purple finches, or goldfinches about your house. Smaller grain will be more acceptable to sparrows, towhees, cat-birds, mourning doves, juncos, pine siskins.

Birdseed mixtures that you buy are made with many different formulas, and by experimenting you may find the most accepta-ble one. A study of several mixtures showed that all contained canary seed and hemp, and most had some sunflower seed and millet. Other ingredients were kaffir corn, milo, maize, hulled oats, wheat, Sudan grass, and baby-chick feed. Some mixtures contain grit and peanut hearts. I notice a tendency now to in-clude rice, a food that is not very popular with my own birds. The birdseed mixtures may be obtained from pet shops, hard-ware stores, and grain and feed stores. Some Audubon or other bird groups offer their own special mixtures. I pay approximately fifteen cents a pound where I live.

Some bird watchers are enthusiastic about baby-chick scratch feed. This can be bought in twenty-five-pound sacks in feed stores and sells for about five cents a pound. It is a fine mixture of corn, wheat, kaffir, millet, oat groats, and milo. Regular scratch feed for hens seems too coarse for many birds.

There are other seeds that birds will eat. Cardinals, for example, will take cantaloupe, squash, pumpkin, and watermelon seeds.

Another popular seed is the peanut. Peanut hearts are sold in certain birdseed mixtures and are relished by cardinals, blue jays, and other birds. Peanut butter has an even wider acceptance. This is a rather expensive item to provide in quantity, and apparently there is no grade of peanut butter that can be bought at a low

WHAT TO FEED BIRDS

WHAT TO FEED BIRDS 45

price, especially for bird food. Certainly the birds do not need the homogenized, creamy-smooth varieties that your own children prefer, but it should be mixed with fat, cracker crumbs, or corn meal to lighten it a bit. Peanut butter may be spread with a knife on the bark of a tree or dispensed in the peanut-butter or suet sticks to be described in Chapter 5 on "Bird Baths and Feeders." Peanut butter appeals to chickadees, sparrows, titmice, starlings, blue jays, and nuthatches.

WATER. Water is essential to birds at all times. One bird bander in Connecticut who banded 874 evening grosbeaks in the winter of 1945–46, using 775 pounds of sunflower seeds in the process, said that warm water between sunrise and noon was almost as essential as seeds in attracting the birds. When the temperature is below freezing, put out warm water twice a day. A few drops of glycerine may keep it from freezing, but you'll have to experiment with the amount you need at various temperatures.

As I watch the robins on hot days gaining very evident satisfaction from bathing, I realize that a cool bath must be as refreshing to a bird as it is cleansing. Sparrows, however, are fond of dust baths, and a few spadefuls of earth turned up at the base of a sunny wall will satisfy their needs.

GRIT. Grit helps birds digest their foods. It is especially necessary in winter, when deep snow covers the ground and birds are not able to reach it otherwise. A dish of sand or coal ashes, placed on a feeding tray, will suffice. Most birdseed mixtures contain some grit; this is also true of chick feeds.

OTHER FOODS. Birds come to like various other foods. Overwintering myrtle warblers that have depleted the local supply of bayberries may visit your feeding station to feed on doughnuts. Other insectivorous birds that arrive early from the south like doughnuts and other fatty substances. Birds that will eat small mixed seeds and peanut butter will also take crumbs of bread, cornbread, cake, and bits of pastry. A woman in Ohio had success with a mixture of corn meal, suet, grease, peanut butter, and greasy noodles that did not freeze. I have had some success with small chunks of bread fried in whatever grease might be left over from cooking.

Pork rinds, chopped pork, shattered dog biscuits, bread soaked in milk, heels of cheese, are other foods that are well received.

Nor should we forget fruit. Fleshy grapes, halves of oranges, with the soft sides up, and halves of apples are taken by orioles, jays, and other birds. Sugar water in small tubes will be relished by hummingbirds. Knowing their predilection for red, I even tried syrup of grenadine one summer and matched the color of the syrup with red plastic containers. I never saw the hummingbirds at this attractive offering, but I have seen them sipping from nearby red bergamot.

List of birds and foods

Some of the more common birds found at feeding stations and some of their favorite foods are as follows:

Blackbirds Sunflower seeds, corn, shelled broken peanuts, scratch feed.
Blue jay Sunflower seed, suet, peanut hearts, cracked nuts, corn.
Bob-white Chicken scratch.
Brown creeper Suet.

Cardinal Sunflower seed, cantaloupe seeds, corn, shelled and broken peanuts, scratch feed.
Catbird Apple, orange, currants, raisins, bread crumbs.
Chickadee Small seeds, sunflower seed, peanut butter, cracked nuts, bread crumbs, suet.

Finches Sunflower seed, millet, scratch feed, wheat, screenings, small-seed mixtures, bread crumbs.

Goldfinch Canary seed, millet.

Hummingbirds Sugar water (one part sugar, two parts water).

Junco Mixed small seeds, milo, scratch feed, wheat, screenings, bread crumbs, millet.

Mockingbird Cut apples, currants, raisins, bread crumbs.
Mourning dove Mixed small seeds.

Nuthatch Suet, sunflower seed, peanut butter, cracked nuts, bread crumbs.

Pheasant Cracked corn.
Purple finch Sunflower and other seeds, such as hemp, millet, and chick feed.

Redpoll Hemp.
Robin Currants, raisins, bread crumbs, cut apples and oranges, short lengths of cooked spaghetti.

Sparrows Mixed small seeds, scratch feed, millet, wheat, screenings, bread crumbs.
Starling Suet, cut apples, currants, scratch feed, table scraps.

Thrushes Cut apples and oranges, currants, raisins, bread crumbs.
Towhee Scratch feed, shelled and broken peanuts, corn.
Titmouse Suet, peanut butter, cracked nuts, sunflower seeds, bread crumbs.

Woodpeckers Suet, cracked nuts, corn.

What to feed baby birds

Every year people telephone me or write me letters about baby birds, or come to my house with young birds in their hands, asking, "What shall I feed it?" In most cases these birds would have been taken care of by their parents if they had been left alone and a watch kept for cats. However, nests are occasionally destroyed or birds orphaned, and intelligent care must be given if the young are to survive. But it is an exacting task to care for an orphaned bird, and the relationship should not be entered into lightly.

Nestlings demand food incessantly, although overfeeding can be harmful. They cannot be fed too much at one time, nor can they be handled excessively. During the first few days feedings should be every fifteen minutes from early morning till dusk; later this schedule may be lengthened to once an hour. Birds like to be fed, but they have to be taught to feed themselves. A woman in California who has had success in rearing baby birds uses for very young nestlings a basic food of equal parts of finely sifted bread crumbs and finely mashed yolk of hard-boiled eggs. Both are slightly moistened with milk. The food is given on the end of a medicine dropper or other thin implement. In about a week she adds to this mixture some finely sifted corn meal for seed-eating birds and finely chopped meat or worms for insect eaters. Additional food should not be put down a bird's throat until it has swallowed the food just given.

At the end of two weeks the birds also receive finely chopped water cress and nasturtium leaves and flowers. These plants are rich in calcium and in vitamins A and C; they also contain some B_1. The diet is further increased with fine gravel or charcoal, crushed seed, chopped greens and fruit, and worms or other insects.

Young birds should not be forced to drink. They can get enough liquid from juicy food, but will choke if water is poured down their throats. When the bird can perch, it will drink from a shallow dish.

For injured birds the best treatment is immobilization of broken bones, with ample feedings of food rich in calcium and vitamins to hasten recovery.

Injured or orphaned birds should be kept in individual cages and released as soon as possible. It is illegal in New Jersey to have wild birds in one's possession. Even to care for birds requires a permit which is canceled when the bird is released.

Food needn't be bought

Bird watchers may find more satisfaction in providing food themselves than in merely buying it over the counter. For instance, weed seeds are a natural bird food. Take a paper bag when you walk in the fields in the fall, and gather seeds of thistle, dock, clover, wild mustard, and other plants. One year there were no jays in our neighborhood from November until April, an absence that I attributed to the poor acorn crop that fall. If you gather an ample store of acorns, you may feed them to these hungry birds in place of sunflower seed, and watch the jays hack open the shells with their sharp bills.

You can dry and clean seeds of squash, pumpkin, gourds, and melons, and expect them to be eaten by chickadees, woodpeckers, nuthatches, and cardinals. Lettuce, radishes, Swiss chard, and turnips will bolt to seed in late summer; if these seeds are dried they will be accepted by sparrows, juncos, and goldfinches. You may also want to let some of your larkspur, cosmos, or other garden flowers go to seed and put them on your feeding trays in the winter for all seed-eating birds. It is fun, too, to grow a few sunflowers and put out the whole heads of seed.

All coniferous trees provide food. When white-winged crossbills invaded our region in spectacular numbers in the winter of 1952–53, I knew I would find the birds around hemlocks, for they are especially fond of the small cones. Almost every stand in our neighborhood attracted some of these rare birds, feeding on trees and ground. You may gather various cones before a frost and dry them in a warm room. They will open, and you can shake the seed into a box or sack. Pine siskins will be especially fond of this food, and in recent winters these Northern birds have come down in substantial numbers. I have also seen them feeding greedily on birch catkins and on the seeds from the spherical fruit of the sweet gum.

SUET CAKES. On occasion my twelve-year-old daughter makes suet cakes for the birds. She gets small paper cartons from the confectioner's and fills them with melted suet, to which she adds raisins, peanut hearts, and birdseed, especially sunflower. You can experiment with this formula, adding hard cereals, chopped nuts, currants, or other ingredients. The downy woodpeckers, chickadees, and titmice are especially avid eaters. Food cakes may be made of corn meal, oatmeal, bread crumbs, chopped peanuts, raisins, mixed with eggs and baked. And don't forget there are many table scraps that birds will eat.

RAISING WORMS. I once raised worms, buying from a concern in Michigan cans of worm spores packed in moss. I planted them in a rich earth in a box in the cellar, feeding them religiously on corn meal and lettuce and other green vegetables and watering them frequently. In this way I had worms in the winter when the outside worm population had retreated several feet under the surface. This is an interesting operation but a rather exacting one, and hardly worth the trouble.

chapter 5 / Bird baths and feeders

We have three kinds of bird baths in our yard. One is a shallow pan placed in a depression in the ground. My daughter made that. Then we bought two cement baths that stand on pedestals. They are shallow, not more than two inches deep in any area, because the birds are afraid of deep water. You may have noticed that birds bathing in a brook always seek shallow edges or little trickles of water. The word *bath* is used here, although *pool* would be as appropriate, for the birds get even more benefit from a source of drinking water than from a place to bathe. These baths are sometimes called *fountains*, even if they do not spout water.

Birds like water in motion. If you put water in a bucket that has a small hole in it, and suspend the bucket over a pool, you will

The drip bird bath

find that the constant dripping attracts birds. A hose can be ad-
justed to allow only a small amount of water to fall into a pool.

We also have a ground-level bird bath or pool. We made it by
scooping out a section of the lawn some 6 feet long, 3 feet wide,
and almost a foot deep. We covered the inside with a layer of
cinders for drainage, and plastered the cinders with concrete about
2 inches thick. We made some of this concrete by mixing four
parts of sand and gravel to one part of cement, with enough
water to make it like thick batter. You can also buy bags of
sand and cement already mixed, so that all you have to do is add
water. This works very well. You can also make a simple pool by
pouring cement into a depression made by a ring of large stones.
Our pool is a great attraction to the birds, especially during the
dry summers that we have suffered in recent years.

One of the finest bird baths I have ever seen is owned by a
friend in a nearby town. It is a flat stone some 6 inches high and
1½ feet in diameter. In the center is a sizable depression. This
stone was used by the Indians to grind corn, and the depression
which once held the corn now holds water for birds.

In placing the bird bath, it is well to have it near a tree or
shrub that leans over the water. Ours is beside some drooping
rose vines. Such a setup is attractive to vireos, flycatchers, and
other birds that like nearby perches and protection. Moreover, a
wet bird cannot fly very far, so if a branch is nearby the bird can

more readily escape enemies. As in placing any feeder, do not put the bath near a stump or post that might provide a hiding place for a cat.

WINDOW-SHELF FEEDER. The simplest type of feeder is the window-shelf tray. It should be fastened to the window sill and might have a shoulder on the outer side to keep the food from falling off. A plain feeding board fastened to the window sill can be made more inviting by tacking evergreen twigs around the edge. This type of feeder can be made a bit more effective by attaching sides and a top. These will protect both food and birds from the elements. If the top is glass, you can get a better view of the feathered guests at your window. I have built such feeders and covered them with ordinary window glass, only to find the glass broken repeatedly by squirrels who come down the drainpipe and land on all fours on the glass top. I have solved this difficulty by using heavier glass. There seems to be no way of protecting this station from squirrels, although I have made other feeders squirrelproof.

SUET FEEDERS. One of the best suet feeders is a crocheted bag that is fastened to a tree or feeder or hung from a branch. I use a string bag that contains the oranges we buy in the supermarket. The simplest and most effective way of dispensing suet is merely

Window-shelf feeder

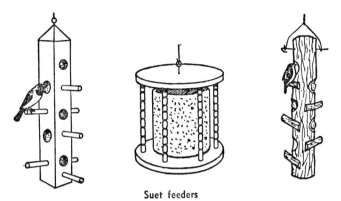

Suet feeders

to fasten it to a tree trunk with several windings of cotton twine. An efficient suet feeder is a short section of branch or stick of wood, from two to four inches thick and bored at frequent intervals with holes approximately an inch in diameter and an inch deep. You can pour melted suet into the holes or merely cram it in with your fingers. Small pieces of wood should be nailed under each hole as perches for birds that are not so agile as woodpeckers. The stick should be suspended from one end and allowed to swing free. White ash and sassafras are good woods for these suet sticks, as the bark is rough and adheres tightly to the sapwood. Birds that ordinarily feed on the bark of trees, such as woodpeckers, creepers, chickadees, and nuthatches, can be counted upon to visit the suet stick regularly. You may fill some of the holes with peanut butter. Suet feeders made of metal, such as soap dishes, have been frowned upon because of the possibility of the birds' freezing their eyes, feathers, or tongues against the metal in sub-zero weather. This danger may be avoided by giving the metal a heavy coating of paraffin. John K. Terres, author of *Songbirds in Your Garden*, tells me he has never known of a case where a bird was so injured. Others have reported such instances, however.

TROLLEY FEEDERS. Trolley feeders are attached to a rope or wire by a trolley. They have two, and possibly three, advantages. They are easy to replenish, as all you have to do is pull the feeder toward you on its rope. They also enable you to pull the feeder gradually nearer your own position once the birds have become accustomed to visiting it. In this way you can bring the birds right to your window. The third possible advantage is that trolley feeders are somewhat more protected from squirrels and cats. If high enough from the ground, they are practically catproof. However, I have found that a squirrel can travel along a very thin wire, so don't count upon this device as much protection against these rodents. Incidentally, almost any kind of hanging feeder can be suspended from a rope run through a pulley fastened to a tree limb, with the other end tied to a boat cleat or awning cleat. Such an arrangement makes it easier to lower the feeders for filling.

POST FEEDERS. I have one feeder that is absolutely squirrel-proof, and I built it myself. I fastened a box-type feeder on top of an 8-foot pipe, and fastened the pipe on a base made of boards nailed together. Then I got an ironworker to cut a cone of galvanized iron that I fastened around the pipe, its down diameter some 2½ feet. The squirrels have never been able to get up the pipe and past the cone. This feeder can be moved from place to place in the yard, and this is sometimes an advantage. Sometimes these post feeders have large inverted paint or oil cans fastened to the top of the pipe or post.

GENERAL CONSIDERATIONS. You can make a simple feeder yourself, or buy any one of a great variety in retail stores or by mail order. They range in price from seventy-five cents to thirty-five dollars. However, a simple structure does perfectly well, and if made of stained oak will become a natural part of the outdoors.

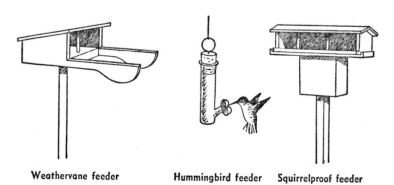

Weathervane feeder   Hummingbird feeder   Squirrelproof feeder

Feeders should be placed where there is little exposure to attacks by cats, and so situated that the birds can make a quick getaway if enemies come. A sheltered spot will prevent the food's being blown out by strong winds and will also afford protection for the birds. Weathervane feeders create their own sheltered lee.

Some feeding stations are fitted with small hoppers that dispense feed as it is eaten. These can be made without trouble, and are recommended, as they conserve seed and keep it clean. There are similar devices for dispensing water.

A heavy storm may present the need to put out much more feed than usual. You can clear a space in the snow and scatter seed, finding that sparrows, cardinals, juncos, grosbeaks, and other ground-feeding birds will feed there. You can also improvise feeders by placing garden flats in crotches of trees. I have had success at such times with discarded wooden fruit boxes. These boxes have a partition down the middle, and when placed on end the partition serves as a shelf. A heavy stone put inside the bottom will prevent the box from blowing over. These boxes provide shelter as well as food.

Control of pests

What is a pest? If a weed, according to definition, is merely a flower out of place, so a pest is a bird or animal out of place. To the bird watcher, cats and squirrels are admirable in their place, but their place is not the sanctuary.

CATS ON THE LOOSE. My correspondents, with occasional violent exceptions, feel that cats that run wild are definite hazards to bird life and should be controlled. It is possible that there are twenty million cats in the United States, and that each cat may kill as many as fifty birds a year. One of my readers tells of seeing a cat jump three feet in the air to knock down an olive-backed thrush, and a physician in a suburb of New York tells of seeing a cat during one week end kill twelve robins on his lawn. Some people seem to keep not one cat, but several. A woman in a neighboring community was charged with harboring fifty of the beasts, and not restraining them from onslaughts on the birds in the vicinity.

Bird watchers should look at their own state laws on the control of cats. In New Jersey, for instance, anyone who has a hunting license is permitted to shoot cats that are found prowling the woods and fields in the act of killing protected species of birds or with the evident intent to do so. This is probably the only feasible kind of state law, for it is impossible to control a cat the way a dog can be controlled. You may require a cat to be licensed, but once you let it loose it may start to kill. It cannot be confined by a leash or by a high fence, as dogs can be confined. The best procedure is to require that cats be belled, and some communities in my state do so require. There are people who keep cats and maintain feeding stations, but it must be a strain on the bird watcher, the cat, and the birds.

GREEDY SQUIRRELS. Squirrels are attractive in many ways, and add to the local color. But they are entirely without conscience in the amount of sunflower seeds they eat. I do not object to a squirrel or two about the place, but a dozen or two become an affliction. My best solution is to get in touch with the State Fish and Game Commission. A warden comes and leaves two box traps. I put an ear of corn in one trap, and as a squirrel walks in, the door drops behind it. Then I transfer the trapped squirrel to the other trap, covering it with a canvas so that the beast will be quieted and will not frighten other possible victims. One winter I captured twelve squirrels this way, and a next-door neighbor caught eleven. The Fish and Game Commission's warden came every other day to take the beasts away, as they fought together in the trap. He took the animals to city parks or state forests, where they were liberated. This thinning of the squirrel population relieved us for some years of the terrible raids we and the birds used to suffer.

I have found that the only real squirrelproof feeding station is the one on a pipe, protected by an inverted cone or big tin can. I put seeds on this feeder that the squirrels like particularly well, and place in feeders available to the squirrels the cheaper feed that they do not take so readily.

MERITS OF HOUSE SPARROWS. I do not object to English sparrows, and neither do most of my readers. The days when these birds were considered "vermin of the air," to be eliminated as rapidly as possible, appear to be on the wane. The house sparrows about my place are very numerous and eat much feed. However, they subsist well enough on inexpensive cracked corn, and I have not found that they eat any substantial amount of sunflower seed. Many people say that sparrows are greedy birds, but what they really mean is that they are aggressive and more successful in finding and holding a place for themselves in an environment than are some of our native species. Certainly their table manners are not more objectionable than those of some more gaudily garbed creatures. The most aggressive bird we have ever had at our feeder, in the sense that it chased other birds that wanted to share the feed, was a scarlet tanager.

Most of my correspondents feel that house sparrows attract other birds to feeding stations. In my region this has been the case with dickcissels, birds that have been quite rare here until the last year or so. They are so sparrowlike in appearance that sometimes they are overlooked until their yellow breasts are noticed. They have almost always been found in the company of house sparrows, and I continually noted my own flocks of sparrows in the hope of finding this Western species among them. Another merit of house sparrows is that they are adding insects to their diet, whereas formerly they insisted on grain. Moreover, the population of the species seems to be somewhat stabilized, as that of the Japanese beetle is becoming stabilized in the areas where it was first established. Actually, the sparrows may help in this process, as my correspondents have told me they have seen house sparrows feeding Japanese beetles to their young.

OTHER PESTS. Seed and other feed scattered on the ground may attract rats, white-footed and house mice, chipmunks, and cottontails, but none of these are likely to constitute a major nuisance. Sharp-shinned hawks, Cooper's hawks, and shrikes are occasional pests, but I have never been bothered with them. Having recently seen a myrtle warbler alight on a branch beside a loggerhead shrike, with neither paying any attention to the other, I have become a little dubious about the fearsome effect on small birds of the so-called "gray death." These predators normally feed upon birds whose reactions are slowed because of deformities, internal parasites, injuries, or old age. The question of whether we should interfere in this process of natural selection or should give protection to the victims and unwittingly help the propagation of an inferior race is a nice question, involved with humanitarian as well as biological considerations. Predators have an important place in nature, preventing the degeneration of species, and keeping animal populations from increasing beyond their limits of food supply. However, the mere presence of predators may keep birds away from feeding stations in severe weather when the birds need food. One solution is to catch the bird of prey in a banding trap and release it in some other area.

Reading reference

Songbirds in Your Garden, by JOHN K. TERRES, Thomas Y. Crowell Company, New York, 1953, 274 pp., illus.

chapter 6 / Nesting boxes and shelters

If you provide nesting boxes and weather shelters as well as food and water, you will become increasingly successful in attracting birds. The government has estimated that the average number of birds in the eastern United States is 1 pair an acre, but that it is possible to increase this number to 10 in suburban areas if bird watchers conduct programs that make their yards more attractive places for their feathered guests.

SPECIES THAT USE NESTING BOXES. There are fifty species of birds of the United States that have been known to nest in bird boxes or on supporting devices such as shelves, according to a count by the Fish and Wildlife Service. They are as follows:

Song sparrow
House finch
Purple grackle
Bullock's oriole
Orchard oriole
House sparrow
Starling
Mountain bluebird
Western bluebird
Eastern bluebird
Robin
Brown thrasher
Mockingbird
Carolina wren
Bewick's wren
House wren
Brown creeper
Red-breasted nuthatch
White-breasted nuthatch
Plain titmouse
Tufted titmouse
Chestnut-backed chickadee
Mountain chickadee
Carolina chickadee
Black-capped chickadee

Blue jay
Purple martin
Cliff swallow
Barn swallow
Tree swallow
Violet-green swallow
Phoebe
Ash-throated flycatcher
Crested flycatcher
Arkansas kingbird
Golden-fronted woodpecker
Downy woodpecker
Red-headed woodpecker
Hairy woodpecker
Red-shafted flicker
Yellow-shafted flicker
Saw-whet owl
Screech owl
Barn owl
Mourning dove
Sparrow hawk
Hooded merganser
American goldeneye
Wood duck
Mallard

GENERAL CONSIDERATIONS. Although you are likely to have more birds nesting around your place if you provide nesting boxes, you will not necessarily have more than one pair of a single species. Birds of the same kind do not ordinarily nest near each other. Most birds that use nesting boxes originally nested in woodpeckers' holes or in other hollows in trees. This is a clue to the construction of such houses. It also indicates that birds do not like square or rectangular entrances. The sparrow that nests most commonly in provided boxes is the house sparrow, which is actually an imported weaver finch. Both house sparrows and starlings are adaptable birds that will preempt other nesting sites, tending to reduce the population of native species in your neighborhood. This is all the more reason to provide homes for birds if you want more birds around your own house.

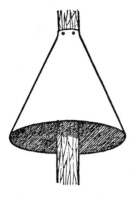

Squirrel guard on tree   Rustic house

PRINCIPLES OF LOCATION. Boxes should be placed so that they can be reached by a ladder for cleaning. Houses placed on poles are more generally used than those placed in trees, because the latter are more accessible to the birds' enemies, such as squirrels, jays, and crows. If the pole has a squirrel guard, it will be safer. Houses should be placed facing the south, and generally should be tilted forward, to protect them as much as possible from driving rains.

PRINCIPLES OF CONSTRUCTION. Nesting boxes should be durable, rainproof, cool, and readily accessible for cleaning. They can also be made attractive. Wood is best, as metal heats in the sun. Woods easily workable, such as cypress, pine, and yellow poplar, are preferable. Sawmill waste, which consists of rough slabs with the bark still on, furnishes cheap and satisfactory material for birdhouses. Wood improves, rather than suffers, from exposure to weather. Although birdhouses, such as martin houses, that are placed in exposed positions, may be painted white to reflect the sun, the best colors are modest tones, such as brown, gray, and green. A rustic finish may be obtained by covering the birdhouse with bark. I generally stain mine brown or allow them to weather so that they acquire a silvery gray. Avoid using too large an auger to bore entrance holes, as the wood may split. It is best to use a 1-inch bit and enlarge the hole with a rasp if necessary.

Nesting shelf   Accessible nesting box

DETAILS OF CONSTRUCTION. For durability, the thickness of the boards used should range between ½ and 1 inch. Roofs should be made with sufficient pitch to shed water; either a tent-shaped roof, or one with a slant to the front if it is flat. The entrance should also be protected from rain, an overhang of 2 to 3 inches proving effective. A strip of metal or roofing paper may be used to keep the ridge of the nesting box waterproof. If the roof is flat, it should be covered with this material or with thick paint to make it waterproof. If the sides are prolonged below the bottom of the box, they will allow water to drain off and prevent its collecting between bottom and sides and freezing.

If the inside of the box becomes overheated in the late spring or early summer, the nestlings may suffocate. A single entrance hole near the top affords little ventilation, so one or two auger holes through the walls near the top of the box will allow air to circulate without producing drafts. These holes also admit light, making the interior less formidable to a bird on its first visit to a prospective home. An excellent insulator may be provided in a double roof or a compartment above the nest proper.

ENTRANCE HOLES, DIMENSIONS. Entrance holes are usually made near the tops of bird houses; hence the wood should be rough with the bark still on it, or else grooved, cleated, or otherwise roughened to help the young birds climb to the opening. Remember that the insides of woodpecker holes are rough. Perches near the entrance are not desirable, as they seem to be less helpful to the bird tenants than to their enemies. Dimensions and elevations aboveground are given in the table on page 64.

CLEANING BIRDHOUSES. Nests must be cleaned regularly, for the benefit of both the birds and the owner. Gypsy and tussock moths place their eggs or cocoons in birdhouses, and they are also invaded by daubers and paper wasps, bees, mice, and flying squirrels. Once wasps become established in a house, the birds will not use it. Insects may be stupefied with fumes of carbon tetrachloride or even smoke. The mammal intruders may be dumped out. Old nesting materials should be burned and the inside of the nesting box swabbed with a household disinfectant.

Houses should be cleaned just before the nesting season and immediately after broods have left, as birds are subject to parasites. Common bird lice are not serious, but blood-sucking flies cause mortality among young birds.

NESTING MATERIALS. Nest building about one's property may be facilitated by the provision of nesting materials, such as excelsior, straw, hay, cotton, short pieces of twine, and thoroughly wet clay. I have placed colored strands of wool for Baltimore orioles, and found them accepted readily. Do not put nesting materials within a house, as the intended occupant may believe it is already occupied and shun it merely to avoid a quarrel.

Robins like soft cotton string or strips of cotton cloth. Cotton batting will be used by wood pewees, kingbirds, and vireos.

PROTECTION OF NESTS. Nesting boxes and nestlings should be protected if possible against cats, dogs, and squirrels, and against other birds such as starlings, crows, and jays. This subject has been treated from another aspect under the subject of "Bird Baths and Feeders," Chapter 5. It is especially desirable to restrain domestic pets, such as cats and dogs, during the nesting season, and vagrant animals must be dealt with summarily. The same kinds of guards that protect feeding stations will also protect nesting boxes if the latter are placed on trees or poles. Multiflora roses at the bases of poles supporting nests will deter pests. Starlings, when overabundant, may preempt nesting places suitable for other birds, especially purple martins.

Dimensions of nesting boxes for various species of regular box-inhabiting birds and the height at which they should be placed above the ground.*

Species	Floor of cavity	Depth of cavity	Entrance above floor	Diameter of entrance	Height above ground [1]
	Inches	Inches	Inches	Inches	Feet
Bluebird	5 × 5	8	6	1½	5–10
Robin	6 × 8	8	([2])	([2])	6–15
Chickadee	4 × 4	8–10	6– 8	1⅛	6–15
Titmouse	4 × 4	8–10	6– 8	1¼	6–15
Nuthatch	4 × 4	8–10	6– 8	1¼	12–20
House wren	4 × 4	6– 8	1– 6	1–1¼	6–10
Bewick's wren	4 × 4	6– 8	1– 6	1–1¼	6–10
Carolina wren	4 × 4	6– 8	1– 6	1½	6–10
Violet-green swallow	5 × 5	6	1– 5	1½	10–15
Tree swallow	5 × 5	6	1– 5	1½	10–15
Barn swallow	6 × 6	6	([2])	([2])	8–12
Purple martin	6 × 6	6	1	2½	15–20
Song sparrow	6 × 6	6	([3])	([3])	1– 3
House finch	6 × 6	6	4	2	8–12
Starling	6 × 6	16–18	14–16	2	10–25
Phoebe	6 × 6	6	([2])	([2])	8–12
Crested flycatcher	6 × 6	8–10	6– 8	2	8–20
Flicker	7 × 7	16–18	14–16	2½	6–20
Golden-fronted woodpecker	6 × 6	12–15	9–12	2	12–20
Red-headed woodpecker	6 × 6	12–15	9–12	2	12–20
Downy woodpecker	4 × 4	8–10	6– 8	1¼	6–20
Hairy woodpecker	6 × 6	12–15	9–12	1½	12–20
Screech owl	8 × 8	12–15	9–12	3	10–30
Saw-whet owl	6 × 6	10–12	8–10	2½	12–20
Barn owl	10 × 18	15–18	4	6	12–18
Sparrow hawk	8 × 8	12–15	9–12	3	10–30
Wood duck	10 × 18	10–24	12–16	4	[4] 10–20

[1] During an experimental birdhouse study, boxes at moderate heights mostly within reach of a man on the ground were readily accepted.

[2] One or more sides open.   [3] All sides open.

[4] Based on experience gained on national wildlife refuges, where approximately 2,500 boxes have been erected for hole-nesting waterfowl.

* Taken from E. R. Kalmbach and W. L. McAtee, "Homes for Birds," Conservation Bulletin No. 14, United States Department of the Interior, Fish and Wildlife Service, Government Printing Office, Washington, 1942, p. 9.

WHEN TO PUT OUT. Fall is the best time to put out nesting boxes, as they thus have time to lose their newness before spring. They may also serve as shelters for winter birds. Spring is the time usually selected, however.

Homes for specific birds

Bluebirds Bluebirds normally nest in abandoned holes of woodpeckers, so a box that simulates such a hole is acceptable. Houses of rustic construction are also acceptable. Bluebirds prefer sunny situations, preferably in orchards. Houses may be placed in trees themselves or on posts that are protected by squirrel guards. The mountain bluebird, Western bluebird, tree swallow, and violet-green swallow will occupy similar boxes.

Robins, catbirds, thrashers Robins will use nesting platforms, although this is more likely in areas where trees and well-formed crotches are lacking. Such nest brackets and shelves should be placed in the shelter of overhanging eaves of a shed or porch roof, or in sheltered spots along the main branches of trees. A shelf 6 to 8 inches wide will suffice for the robin. If you want to know where to place such a shelf, look where robins have built their nests in the past; it may be 6 to 40 feet aboveground. The robin will find its own nesting materials, generally mud and grass, although in a drought it will be helpful to provide a supply of mud so the bird can use it.

Chickadees, titmice, and nuthatches In their natural state, these birds also use abandoned woodpecker holes, so they will nest in a box similar to that provided for the bluebird. They prefer rustic homes, but will accept weathered lumber. Rustic homes such as that shown on page 61 or that shown on page 66, if covered with bark, will be used. If there is a wooded lot nearby, put the nesting box on its edge. Otherwise choose a quiet corner of your yard. Nuthatches like knotholes in trees, so a house made of a hollowed trunk may attract this bird.

Warblers and creepers Brown creepers have been known to nest behind curved pieces of bark fastened to the trunk of a tree, so it is possible they may favor the rustic box featured below. It is thought the parula warbler may also nest in such a site.

Wrens Almost any kind of cavity will meet the nesting needs of the house, Carolina, and Bewick's wrens. Indeed, wrens have been known to nest in

Rustic house with slabs

fantastic places, such as the pockets of clothes hanging on a line or on scarecrows in the cornfields. Small boxes with a horizontal slit near the top instead of a hole seem best. This is because wrens like to carry in a jumble of sticks whenever they can. The slot or hole may be 1 to 1¼ inches in diameter, instead of the often used ⅞-inch size, although this runs the danger of preemption by house sparrows. The slightly larger opening may be more suitable for the Carolina wren, as this is a larger bird. Both house and Bewick's wrens prefer sunny situations, although I have seen a house placed in full shade that has been occupied by house wrens year after year.

Swallows Other birds that sometimes nest in woodpecker holes are tree and violet-green swallows; hence they may be induced to use the boxes shown on pages 61 and 62. A number of such nests may be attached to a dead tree, and the operation will be especially successful if the tree is near a small body of water.

Open or partly covered nest shelves will be accepted by barn swallows if the shelves are placed under the protective eaves of buildings. Narrow cleats nailed horizontally to rafters, with access to them afforded by an opening in the gable, will satisfy this species.

Purple martins There are not many places in my region where purple martins nest, but in nearby Morristown there is a spot where they have returned annually a great many years. The site of their choice is a large martin house. On page 68 is shown how such houses may be constructed. Each story is made a unit, and the uniform size permits the addition of other stories as needed. No more than two dozen martins are normally contained in one colony; a colony may be started with one story of eight rooms. The house is held together with hooks and screw eyes, so it may be cleaned by taking it apart. Inside temperature is kept down by air circulated through the passage formed by cutting out the floors of what would otherwise be central apartments. Passage of air is also facilitated by raising the roof slightly above the top of the central section. Houses for martins should be situated in the open and painted white to reflect the heat. A pond or other body of water nearby increases the likelihood of a martin colony's being established in your neighborhood. Wood for the walls and floors should be ¾ inch thick, that for the roof and interior partitions ½ inch thick. (Plan designed by Fish and Wildlife Service.)

The Chattanooga Audubon Society in Tennessee has a unique method of attracting purple martins. The Society is operating under the slogan, "A colony of martins for every country and suburban home." Seventy-five years ago many rural residences in this state had a few gourds suspended from a crossbeam anchored to the top of an upright pole in an open space. The gourds were favored by the martins. However, the gourd homes gradually disappeared as country people moved to the city. In 1951 the Society erected a handsome martin house, but it went untenanted. The next year it put out fifty gourds, cut with holes 2 inches wide but high enough in the gourd to keep the baby martins from falling out. Three holes the size of a pencil were bored in the gourd bottoms to permit drainage of water. The gourds were placed on two stout wires parallel to each other between strong posts and were painted white. These homes were readily accepted by the birds. The Society announced a free distribution of gourd seeds to anyone who would agree to plant and grow them purposely to attract martins. It distributed 60,000 seeds, with requests coming from as far away as Pennsylvania and California. I saw one of these beams with gourds for martins in Summerville, South Carolina, a few years ago.

Gourd martin houses

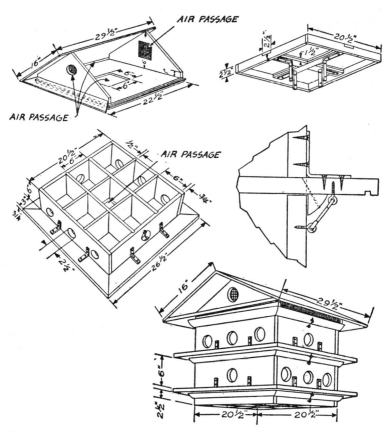

Construction details of martin house. Foundation, roof, and each story are built as separate units of uniform lateral dimensions, permitting addition of more stories as needed, also easy cleaning. Central airshaft and elevated roof, permitting passage of air beneath eaves, assure cooler interior. Molding around underside of roof and each story holds parts aligned; pairs of hooks and eyes fasten units together.

Top left: roof with one side removed to show central airshaft. Air also passes through 1-inch slot under the eaves and through two screened holes in the ends. Center left: one of the stories. Chambers are 6 by 6 by 6 inches, inside dimensions, and bottom of central chamber is cut out. Top right: foundation, in which central cross is built up of double thicknesses of ¾-inch oak and rest of frame is of ¾-inch pine. Four heavy angle irons fasten this to supporting pole. Center right: detail of porch when attached with angle irons. The molding fits about top of lower story; groove or under edge prevents water from draining inward. This plan may be modified by attaching floors and porches to top, rather than bottom, of each story, facilitating cleaning at season's end but precluding possibility of evicting undesirable tenants once nesting has started. Bottom: assembled house.

Song sparrows These birds may be attracted by placing near a thicket a covered nest shelf, painted in some neutral hue.

Phoebes Phoebes, like swallows, prefer to be near water. Hence they like to nest on the broad timbers beneath a bridge. They may be attracted away from their natural haunts by nesting shelves 5 to 6 inches wide. The shelf should be placed 8 to 12 feet high. Phoebes like a roof close over their nests.

Crested flycatcher Crested flycatchers normally nest in hollows in trees or in abandoned woodpecker holes. Hence they may be attracted by boxes of weathered or painted lumber or made from slabs of natural wood with the bark remaining. The latter type is more successful than the homes made of finished lumber. They should be placed in orchards, in open woodland, or in trees in pastures.

Woodpeckers Boxes made to the proper dimensions and conforming to that illustrated on page 62 are acceptable to woodpeckers. Painted or weathered lumber is satisfactory, but roughened or natural wood interiors are preferred, as they help the young birds to climb to the entrance. Sawdust or small chips placed in the interior to a depth of one or two inches help the bird shape a cavity for eggs. A dead stump or a pole that enables the box to be elevated above surrounding foliage is desirable. A section of a hollow trunk may be transformed into a flicker house. The nesting box should not be placed too near a residence.

Downy and hairy woodpeckers occupy similar houses, their needs varying only in size of nest cavity and entrance. Boxes of the type shown on page 62 are acceptable, and should be placed in an orchard or in open woodland.

Owls The woodpecker type of box illustrated on page 62 is also acceptable to screech owls if made of weathered lumber of the proper size and stained a drab color or covered with bark. The boxes should be placed in an orchard or wood lot. Barn owls will also nest in this type of box if it is made in the proper size. The boxes should be placed on the trunks of large trees or in secluded spots on buildings.

Wood ducks Nail kegs with large round openings make suitable nests for wood ducks. The kegs should be fastened to the trunks of trees, preferably a quarter to a half mile from water. A box of the type on page 62, of proper dimensions, is also accepted. Sawdust or rotten wood should be placed in the bottom to a depth of four inches or so. Wood ducks do not like to nest very near water because of predatory raccoons that inhabit such areas. However, this preference is not rigid, as I have seen the nests right over water.

Shelters

Birds need not only places to nest, but also spots where they can find shelter against wind and storm.

BRUSH PILE. Every fall I make a large brush pile in my yard, and it is greatly favored by the birds. They hide in it at night and during bad weather, perch on it during sunny days, and fly into it when startled. I merely collect some large boughs from adjoining woods and pile smaller branches on them. On the top I mass leaves or lay branches of evergreens, so that the covering is proof against rain and snow. The birds love it. I burn the brush pile in April.

CHRISTMAS-TREE PILE. After each Christmas I collect evergreen trees from my neighbors, and sometimes have half a dozen. I pile these together on the ground, fastening them so that they do not blow away. These also make a fine winter shelter.

HILLSIDE SHELTER. A good shelter under which small game such as bob-whites and pheasants can be fed and sheltered can be built

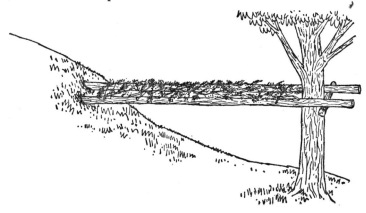

Sidehill shelter

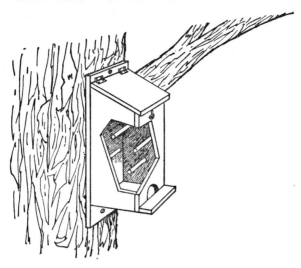

Roosting box

quite easily. Fasten a good-sized pole horizontally between two trees 3 to 4 feet aboveground. Then lay a series of parallel smaller poles from the horizontal pole to the higher ground in the rear of the two trees. Cover these poles with hemlock or pine branches, or with brush and weeds, and you have provided a practical and effective shelter, three of whose sides are open. The frame may be covered with building or roofing paper, then hemlock or pine branches over the paper. The paper will last throughout the winter and will help protect the grain from rain and snow. You may place corn or other grain or scratch feed under the shelter.

ROOSTING BOXES. The removal of hollow trees and thickets has increased the need for roosts in which birds can find shelter on cold and stormy nights. A typical roost is depicted on this page. These roosting boxes should be waterproof and should be firmly attached to their supports. A southern exposure and a height of 8 to 10 feet above the ground will satisfy most birds. The entrance need not be at the top, as a lower entrance will let what warmth accumulates rise to the top of the shelter and stay there. Perches within should be arranged so that none is directly over another. A box 8 or 10 inches square and 3 feet high will shelter several small birds. An entrance hole 3 inches in diameter will satisfy the smaller birds, while owls should be provided individual boxes with larger openings. Sanitation and protection should be cared for as with nesting boxes.

Reading references

Homes for Birds, by E. R. KALMBACH and W. L. McATEE, United States Department of the Interior, Fish and Wildlife Service, Conservation Bulletin No. 14, United States Government Printing Office, Washington, D.C., 1942, 24 pp. and diagrams.

Bird Houses, Baths and Feeding Shelters, by EDMUND J. SAWYER, Cranbrook Institute of Science, Bloomfield Hills, Michigan, 1944, 35 pp. and diagrams.

Audubon Guide to Attracting Birds, edited by JOHN H. BAKER, Halcyon House, New York, 1943.

Birds in Your Backyard, by TED S. PETTIT, Harper & Bros., New York, 1949, 210 pp., photographs, and line drawings.

Birds will be attracted to a city apartment, a suburban house, or a farm if there are plants that give them food and shelter—in addition to the suet or birdseed that may be provided at feeding stations and to the shelter that may be given by constructed brush piles, windbreaks, hillside shelters, roosts, and other devices.

A great deal has been written on this subject, but most of the original research has been done by the Federal Fish and Wildlife Service and has been published in a series of bulletins written by W. L. McAtee, technical adviser in the office of the director of the Service.

An attempt will be made here to discuss only the principles involved, and to list the plants that will grow anywhere in the United States. For more specific information the reader is referred to bulletins issued by the federal government or to his state agricultural department. For information on growing conditions and culture of the plants in question the reader is referred to the multitude of books on gardening.

The plants that might be added to a person's home grounds in order to attract birds should also be considered in the layout of public and private grounds such as roadside plantings, rights of way, community parking grounds, picnic and fair grounds and public parks, school and college grounds, golf courses, cemeteries, reservoirs. Not everyone is in a position to influence the plantings at such places, but many are, and if they give considered thought to plantings that will attract birds we will make a substantial gain for our bird population.

Plants for food

Plants set out for food should supply seeds and fruit, and also flowers that are visited by hummingbirds. Such plantings will increase the bird population around your house or farm, but they are not really needed by the birds for food until late winter or early spring. Plants that bear long-persisting fruits are juniper, hackberry, thorn apple, flowering apple, mountain ash, holly, Virginia creeper, dogwood, sour gum, persimmon, snowberry, and bush honeysuckle.

FRUITS FOR BIRDS. There are a great many birds that eat fruits but not seeds; many of these are the species that eat insects. Thrushes, flickers, kingbirds, catbirds, and scores more will take fruit provided for them on plantings around the house.

Raspberries, blackberries, and elderberries are most popular with birds, being taken by 100 or more species. However, many gardeners are more concerned with preventing birds from eating these fruits than encouraging them to do so. I have a good stand of red raspberries that become ripe early in July, but see no reason for the robins to eat these or my blueberries that ripen later. There is plenty of other wild animal and vegetable food about for them to eat. I am glad that they like the elderberries, however, for these grow wild in the woods and I don't like them raw myself.

There are 50 to 99 species that like the juniper and red cedar genus, also bayberry, mulberry, pokeberry, strawberry, sumac, grape, dogwood, and blueberry. It makes no sense to me to plant strawberries, blueberries, or grapes for birds, because this is too expensive a food. I know a man who grows strawberries on his estate in Scarsdale, New York, and figures that with overhead and taxes they cost about two dollars a quart. Too expensive a fare for birds. However, juniper and red cedar are excellent decorative plants, and their berries are not good for anything but bird food. There seems little point in planting bayberry for bird food because there is so much of it wild, and the same applies to pokeberry and sumac.

A mulberry tree is something else again. When I was a boy in Alabama we had mulberry trees in our yard, and they provided the finest attraction imaginable for birds. There is a white mulberry tree not far from where I live, and it is always an experience to visit it in the summer, because it is alive with robins, catbirds, wood thrushes, and cardinals. Mulberry trees are rather untidy, but they are worth their weight in birds. Another fully admirable tree is the dogwood. Its berries persist through the winter and are there when the birds need them. The tree is otherwise attractive with its white flowers in the spring and bronze and scarlet leaves in the fall.

From 35 to 49 species of birds take the following long list of plants: greenbrier, hackberry, crab and flowering apple genus, juneberry, thorn apple, rose, crowberry, holly, Virginia creeper, sour gum, bearberry and manzanita genus, huckleberry, snowberry, and viburnum (blackhaw, cranberry bush, and others).

The table shows the fleshy fruits most attractive to birds throughout the United States. With an eye to the farmer, the Fish and Wildlife Service, which compiled this list, has omitted barberries, buckthorns, and currants, because they serve as alternate hosts of rusts attacking wheat, oats, and white pine. Yews, wild cherries, and nightshades are also omitted as being dangerous stock-poisoning plants. However, most suburban yards seem to have barberries, and I like the plant for its attractive appearance and for the food it provides the birds. I recall one late, wet spring when insect food had not developed adequately and the Baltimore orioles relished the barberries that still clung to the plants from the previous fall. Since I have no wheat, oats, or white pine in my neighborhood, I see no reason why I should not plant more barberry, and am doing so. Likewise, there being no stock around to eat the yews (and it would be an expensive meal if they did) I shall continue to plant these attractive evergreens.

Groups of fleshy fruits [1] most attractive to birds throughout the United States [*]

Name of fruit [2]

Common	Generic	Number [3]	Desirable kinds of birds known to eat the fruit [4]
Juniper; red cedar [5]	Juniperus	54	Ruffed and sharp-tailed grouse, bob-white, Eastern flicker, mockingbird, robin, Eastern bluebird, cedar wax-wing, myrtle warbler, evening and pine grosbeaks, purple finch.
Greenbrier	Smilax	44	Ruffed and sharp-tailed grouse, bob-white, wild turkey, Eastern flicker, red-bellied woodpecker, mocking-bird, catbird, brown thrasher, robin, hermit thrush, cardinal.
Bayberry	Myrica	86	Ruffed grouse, bob-white, Eastern flicker, red-bellied and downy woodpeckers, Eastern phoebe, tree swallow, black-capped chickadee, Carolina wren, catbird, brown thrasher, hermit thrush, Eastern bluebird, white-eyed vireo, myrtle warbler, meadowlark, Eastern towhee.

[1] Barberries (Berberis), buckthorns (Rhamnus) and currants (Ribes) are omitted because they serve as alternate hosts of rusts, attacking wheat, oats, and white pine respectively. Yews (Taxus), wild cherries (Prunus), and nightshades (Solanum) also are omitted as being dangerous stock-poisoning plants.

[2] Only those listed that have been found in the stomachs of 10 or more wild species of birds.

[3] Based on records of stomach analyses made by the Fish and Wildlife Service.

[4] Based on both stomach analyses and field observations.

[5] Carries apple rust; should not be planted near valuable orchards.

[*] W. L. McAtee, "Local Bird Refuges," Fish and Wildlife Service Conservation Bulletin 17, U.S. Government Printing Office, Washington, 1942, pp. 9-11.

Groups of fleshy fruits most attractive to birds throughout the United States (*Continued*)

| Name of fruit | | | |
Common	Generic	Number	Desirable kinds of birds known to eat the fruit
Hackberry	Celtis	48	Gambel's and scaled quails, Eastern flicker, yellow-bellied sapsucker, mockingbird, brown thrasher, robin, hermit thrush, Eastern bluebird, cedar waxwing, cardinal.
Mulberry [6]	Morus	44	Yellow-billed cuckoo, red-bellied, red-headed and downy woodpeckers, Eastern kingbird, mockingbird, catbird, robin, wood thrush, cedar waxwing, red-eyed vireo, yellow warbler, orchard and Baltimore orioles, scarlet tanager, cardinal, purple finch.
Pokeberry	Phytolacca	53	Bob-white, mourning dove, Eastern flicker, Eastern kingbird, mockingbird, catbird, robin, hermit, olive-backed, and gray-cheeked thrushes, Eastern bluebird, cardinal, Eastern towhee.
Sassafras	Sassafras	19	Bob-white, Eastern kingbird, catbird, robin, veery, red-eyed vireo.
Spicebush	Benzoin	17	Bob-white, Eastern kingbird, catbird, wood thrush, veery, red-eyed vireo.
Apple	Malus	44	Ruffed grouse, bob-white, ring-necked pheasant, Eastern flicker, red-headed and Lewis' woodpeckers, mockingbird, robin, cedar waxwing, purple finch, pine grosbeak, red crossbill.

[6] Most birds eat mulberries. A list of 26 species observed to do so in Washington, D.C., was published in the report for 1890 (p. 285) of the Ornithologist and Mammalogist to the Secretary of Agriculture. A good many of the species are additional to those in the stomachs of which mulberries have been found.

Groups of fleshy fruits most attractive to birds throughout the United States (*Continued*)

Name of fruit		Num-	Desirable kinds of birds
Common	Generic	ber	known to eat the fruit
Chokeberry	Aronia	19	Ruffed and sharp-tailed grouse, bob-white, brown thrasher, meadowlark.
Mountain-ash	Sorbus	14	Ruffed and sharp-tailed grouse, red-headed woodpecker, catbird, brown thrasher, robin, Bohemian and cedar waxwings, Baltimore oriole, evening and pine grosbeaks.
Juneberry	Amelanchier	42	Eastern flicker, red-headed woodpecker, catbird, robin, hermit thrush, veery, cedar waxwing, Baltimore oriole.
Hawthorn	Crataegus	39	Ruffed grouse, bob-white, robin, purple finch, pine grosbeak.
Strawberry	Fragaria	53	Ruffed grouse, catbird, brown thrasher, robin, wood thrush, cedar waxwing, Eastern towhee.
Raspberry, blackberry	Rubus	149	Ruffed and sharp-tailed grouse, bob-white, Eastern flicker, red-headed woodpecker, Eastern kingbird, tufted titmouse, wren tit, mockingbird, catbird, brown thrasher, robin, wood and olive-backed thrushes, Eastern bluebird, cedar waxwing, red-eyed vireo, orchard and Baltimore orioles, cardinal, rose-breasted, black-headed, and pine grosbeaks, Eastern, spotted, and brown towhees, white-throated, fox, and song sparrows.
Rose	Rosa	42	Ruffed and sharp-tailed grouse, greater prairie chicken, and bob-white.
Crowberry	Empetrum	42	Ruffed grouse, pine grosbeak, tree sparrow, snow bunting.

Groups of fleshy fruits most attractive to birds throughout the United States (*Continued*)

Name of fruit		Num-	Desirable kinds of birds
Common	Generic	ber	known to eat the fruit
Sumac [7]	Rhus	98	Ruffed grouse, bob-white, valley quail, wild turkey, Eastern and Western flickers, red-headed and downy woodpeckers, phoebe, black-capped and Carolina chickadees, wren tit, Carolina wren, mockingbird, catbird, brown and California thrashers, robin, hermit and olive-backed thrushes, Eastern bluebird, white-eyed vireo, Audubon's warbler, goldfinch, Eastern towhee, golden-crowned sparrow.
Peppertree	Schinus	11	Robin, varied and hermit thrushes, cedar waxwing, phainopepla.
Holly	Ilex	49	Ruffed grouse, bob-white, valley quail, Eastern flicker, mockingbird, catbird, brown thrasher, robin, hermit thrush, Eastern bluebird, cedar waxwing.
Supplejack	Berchemia	16	Mockingbird, robin.
Grape	Vitis	89	Ruffed grouse, bob-white, wild turkey, Eastern and red-shafted flickers, red-bellied woodpecker, Eastern kingbird, mockingbird, catbird, brown thrasher, robin, wood thrush, veery, Eastern and Western bluebirds, cedar waxwing, cardinal.
Virginia creeper	Parthenocissus	39	Ruffed grouse, bob-white, Eastern flicker, red-bellied and red-headed woodpeckers, tufted titmouse, mockingbird, brown thrasher, robin, hermit, olive-backed, and gray-cheeked thrushes, Eastern bluebird,

[7] Only nonpoisonous species are considered.

Groups of fleshy fruits most attractive to birds throughout the United States (*Continued*)

Name of fruit		Num-ber	Desirable kinds of birds known to eat the fruit
Common	**Generic**		
			red-eyed vireo, scarlet tanager, evening grosbeak, purple finch.
Buffaloberry	Shepherdia	19	Ruffed and sharp-tailed grouse, mockingbird, hermit thrush, pine grosbeak.
Wild sarsaparilla	Aralia	18	Ruffed grouse, bob-white, robin.
Dogwood	Cornus	98	Ruffed and sharp-tailed grouse, bob-white, Eastern and Western flickers, downy woodpecker, Eastern kingbird, catbird, brown thrasher, robin, hermit, wood, olive-backed, and gray-cheeked thrushes, veery, Eastern bluebird, cedar waxwing, red-eyed and warbling vireos, cardinal, evening and pine grosbeaks, purple finch, white-throated and song sparrows.
Sour gum, tupelo	Nyssa	40	Ruffed grouse, bob-white, wild turkey, Eastern flicker, brown thrasher, robin, olive-backed and gray-cheeked thrushes, Eastern bluebird, cedar waxwing, purple finch.
Wintergreen	Gaultheria	11	Ruffed and sharp-tailed grouse, wren tit.
Bearberry, manzanita	Arctostaphylos	34	Dusky and ruffed grouse, valley and mountain quails, band-tailed pigeon, wren tit, fox sparrow.
Huckleberry	Gaylussacia	48	Ruffed grouse, robin, pine grosbeak, Eastern towhee.
Blueberry	Vaccinium	93	Ruffed grouse, greater prairie chicken, sharp-tailed grouse, bob-white, valley quail, wild turkey, Eastern kingbird, black-capped

Groups of fleshy fruits most attractive to birds throughout the United States (*Continued*)

Name of fruit			
Common	Generic	Number	Desirable kinds of birds known to eat the fruit
			chickadee, tufted titmouse, catbird, brown thrasher, robin, hermit thrush, Eastern bluebird, cedar waxwing, orchard oriole, cardinal, pine grosbeak, Eastern towhee, tree sparrow.
Beautyberry	Callicarpa	11	Bob-white, mockingbird, brown thrasher.
Partridgeberry	Mitchella	10	Ruffed grouse, bob-white.
Honeysuckle	Lonicera	20	Bob-white, catbird, brown thrasher, robin, hermit and olive-backed thrushes, pine grosbeak, white-throated sparrow.
Snowberry, coralberry	Symphoricarpos	36	Ruffed and sharp-tailed grouse, bob-white, valley quail, varied thrush, evening and pine grosbeaks.
Blackhaw, cranberry bush	Viburnum	35	Ruffed and sharp-tailed grouse, yellow-billed cuckoo, Eastern flicker, catbird, brown thrasher, robin, Eastern bluebird, cedar waxwing, purple finch, pine and rose-breasted grosbeaks, and the common redpoll.
Elderberry	Sambucus	120	Ruffed grouse, valley quail, Eastern flicker, red-headed woodpecker, Eastern and Arkansas kingbirds, black phoebe, wren tit, mockingbird, catbird, brown and California thrashers, robin, olive-backed thrush, Eastern and Western bluebirds, phainopepla, red-eyed vireo, rose-breasted and black-headed grosbeaks, brown towhee, white-crowned sparrow.

Seeds for birds

There is also a large group of birds that eat seeds, the sparrows, goldfinches, siskins, juncos, cardinals, evening grosbeaks, and so on. It seems to me that the average bird watcher can reasonably plant alders and birches and other trees about his place, for these provide seeds for birds and also serve other useful purposes. But it is not feasible to plant areas with millets and similar seeds unless one has considerable land, as if he lives on a farm, for instance, or operates a wildlife refuge of considerable extent. Neither does it appeal very much to me to plant garden flowers for the essential purpose of providing birdseed or to allow many of these plants to go to seed after they have borne their flowers. Too much has to be done in the average flower garden to allow it to stand idle for birdseed. Plants have to be cultivated, transplanted, mulched, cut down, and given other attentions. It is much more practicable for the bird watcher who also has a garden to buy the seeds he needs, rather than try to grow them. Here, however, are the findings of the Fish and Wildlife Service in respect to plants for seed eaters:

GARDEN ANNUALS. The following cultivated annual plants belong to the same groups as those upon which the birds feed in nature, and produce good crops of seeds: Prince's feather (Amaranthus hypochondriacus), love-lies-bleeding (A. candatus), asters, rock purslanes (Calandrinia), blessed thistle (Cincus benedictus), centaureas, California poppies (Eschscholtzia), cosmos, marigold, sunflowers, tarweed (Madia elegans), forget-me-nots, portulaca, silene, varieties of sorghum (kaffir, milo, sorgo, and others), and zinnia.

TREE SEEDS. Pine grosbeaks like to eat maple seeds on the ground under the trees, twirling the winged seeds in their bills and biting out the kernels. They are also partial to mountain ash, which retains its berries well into the winter. On their visits to the United States, crossbills show their fondness for the seeds of the arbor vitae, tamarack, various spruces, firs, and pines. The peculiar structure and strength of their bills enables them to tear open the cones and eat the seeds. I remember one year when there was a great invasion of white-winged crossbills in New Jersey, and how avidly the birds fed upon hemlock cones, both on the trees and on the ground beneath. The pine siskins feed on the seeds of white cedar, tamarack, and pines and spruces. I have also seen them eating seeds from the catkins of gray birches and from the spherical seed heads of sweet gum trees.

The blue jay's preference for acorns and beechnuts is well known, and sometimes its distribution in winter is determined by the abundance of this vegetable food. Evening grosbeaks, in their irregular invasions, feed on the seeds of maple, elder, box elder, and ash. Elms, which produce an early crop of tree seeds, are visited by goldfinches and purple finches. The latter birds also seek during winter the seeds from the catkins borne by alders and birches.

FLOWERS FOR BIRDS. Flowers that are notably attractive to hummingbirds are day lilies (Hemerocallis), lilies (Lilium), cannas, bouncing Bet (Saponaria officinalis), spiderflower (Cleome), silktree (Albizzia), red buckeye (Aesculus pavia), morning-glories (Ipomoea), petunias, bee balms (Monarda), scarlet sage (Salvia splendens), and honeysuckles (Lonicera). Jewelweed (Impatiens biflora) and trumpet creeper (Bigonia radicans) are other well-known favorites.

Plants for protection

One big difference between the suburban areas and the woodlands is that while the former have an ample supply of trees, they badly lack underbrush. Birds like the latter for both nest building and protection from the elements and their enemies. Plantings around one's house can give birds this needed shelter. Clumps of shrubbery, luxuriant vines in a few tangled thickets, well-grassed sunny openings, and mature trees combine to make a place where birds can live and prosper. Sunlight and shade, cover and food, water and safety are the essentials for attracting birds. Choice of plants for landscaping may well be made from those useful in providing cover, food, and other necessaries of bird life.

Robins must have trees with fair-sized branches to support their nests, although they often accept such substitutes as nesting shelves. Mockingbirds, catbirds, thrashers, and cardinals require shrubbery for shelter and nesting sites. Shrubs should be allowed to form thickets, and should be pruned back severely when young so that they will produce numerous crotches suitable for supporting nests.

Evergreens have an especial attraction for grackles and jays, but other birds seek their shelter. I have made it a practice to buy a live evergreen tree each Christmas, one year a spruce, hemlocks in other years, and so on, and to set them out in the yard. In this way I have accumulated several evergreens that are growing well, and not only prove attractive as plantings but also provide shelter for birds.

Mature trees with a large and varied insect population attract orioles, vireos, and warblers, and also titmice, chickadees, nuthatches, and woodpeckers, especially the last four groups if the trees are not too carefully groomed.

Reading references

The basic research in this field is found in government publications:

Local Bird Refuges, by W. L. McAtee, United States Department of the Interior, Fish and Wildlife Service, Conservation Bulletin 17, United States Government Printing Office, Washington, D.C., 1942, 17 pp.

Attracting Birds, by W. L. McAtee, United States Department of the Interior, Fish and Wildlife Service, Conservation Bulletin No. 1, United States Government Printing Office, Washington, D.C., 1947, 13 pp.

Plants Useful in Upland Wildlife Management, by W. L. McAtee, Conservation Bulletin No. 7, Fish and Wildlife Service, Washington, D.C., 1941, 50 pp. This bulletin recommends plants suitable for use in attracting birds in ten regions of the United States: Northwestern States, Rocky Mountain States, Northern Plains States, Northeastern States, California, Great Basin States,

Southwestern States, Southern Plains States, Southeastern States, Florida.

Birds in the Garden, by MARGARET MCKENNY, Grosset & Dunlap, New York, 1939, 349 pp. with 32 pages of photographs and 48 color plates.

American Wildlife & Plants: A Guide to Wildlife Food Habits, by ALEXANDER C. MARTIN, HERBERT S. ZIM, and ARNOLD L. NELSON, McGraw-Hill Book Company, Inc., New York, 1951, 500 pp., illus., maps.

chapter 8 / What about glasses?

What kind of glasses you buy depends upon the kind of birding you want to do and upon your personal characteristics and preferences.

If your bird watching is done largely in your own yard, a simple field glass that magnifies three or four times may be entirely adequate. If you are going on field trips, you will find prism binoculars necessary. The 7 x 35 binocular, that magnifies objects seven times, is most popular among bird watchers, and is the best glass for general use. However, if you are going to do certain special types of bird watching, such as observing birds passing the moon or watching ducks on reservoirs or birds at sea, then you can hardly get along without a telescope.

Of course, it is not absolutely necessary to use glasses of any kind. When I started watching birds as a boy, I had no glasses and was shortsighted besides. However, I was agile, and made up in stalking ability for what I lacked in optical aids. My first glass was a crude pair of pocket lenses mounted on an open frame, with a magnification of approximately two times. I am amazed at what I saw then with this very crude equipment.

WHAT IS A TELESCOPE? Any description of different kinds of glasses generally starts with the telescope, as that was the first type invented. A simple telescope, consisting of only two lenses, was invented by Galileo in 1609, and is still used. This instrument has a positive objective lens (the large lens that points toward the object being viewed) and a negative eyepiece lens. The first lens admits the rays of light that come from the object, and converges them toward a focal point in the barrel of the telescope. Before they form a real image they are intercepted by the negative eyepiece. They emerge to strike the eye of the viewer as parallel rays, and present a magnified, erect image. This is called the Galilean telescope.

In 1851, Ignazio Porro, an Italian engineer, developed the first prism telescope. In such a telescope the light passes through the objective lens, and is reflected by the first prism into a second prism, which is set at an opposing angle. The light is then reflected through the eyepiece, and the eye sees an erect, magnified image. This construction shortens the length of the instrument, because the light waves are in effect folded as they go through the instrument instead of passing through in a straight line.

For bird watching and casual astronomical work there are available prismatic telescopes that magnify objects twenty times and can be focused by the mere turning of a knob. Additional eyepieces can be obtained that permit magnification of forty and sixty times. These telescopes have to be used on a tripod or stand. I have found that the two latter magnifications are useful only if the light is excellent, as it is on a bright day at the shore. One type of telescope has a dust cap for each end, so that it is in effect its own carrying case. Telescopes can be bought with objective lenses of 60 or 80 millimeters (25.4 millimeters equal 1 inch).

WHAT IS A FIELD GLASS? If you take a small pair of Galilean telescopes and put them together, you have a field glass. It is a kind of hand-held double telescope. Only four lenses are involved, two for each eye. It is seldom made to magnify more than five times, because otherwise it would be excessively large and heavy. Generally the magnifying power is from two to four. The field of view is narrow as compared with that of the prism binocular. The opera glass is a kind of Galilean field glass.

Field glasses are easy to use and relatively inexpensive. For that reason they are good for children who are just learning to know the birds. They also suffice for watching birds from a window, where the object is close and a high magnification unnecessary. I keep a pair of field glasses in my kitchen, so that they can be picked up quickly if a strange bird appears at one of the feeding stations. However, even for back-yard bird watching you will need binoculars if you begin to look for warblers or other birds high up in the trees.

WHAT IS A BINOCULAR? The prism binocular is a pair of prism telescopes, just as the Galilean field glass is a pair of Galilean telescopes. The first prism binocular was developed by Ernest Abbé in 1893. Two prisms in each barrel of the binocular cause the path of light to zigzag or fold upon itself. This shortens the space between the objective lens and the eyepiece, thus reducing the size of the instrument. This, in turn, allows the prism binocular, in comparison with the Galilean type of field glass, to have a higher range of magnification and a much larger field of vision.

Motion of the binocular is magnified as much as the size of the objects seen. This makes it difficult to use glasses that magnify ten times or more, because they are comparatively heavy and difficult to hold, and any wavering will cause a jumpiness in the image. A strong wind increases the difficulty of holding a heavy binocular steady. It is best to use a telescope with a stand or employ a support for binoculars of such high magnification.

WHAT IS MAGNIFICATION? *Magnification*, or *power*, means the number of times the bird or other object seen through the glass is larger than it appears to the naked eye. Or, to put it another way, the number of times nearer the object seems to be to you. You can usually tell the magnification of a pair of glasses from figures stamped on them. You will see such figures as 7X, 35, or 7 x 35 pressed into the metal, for instance. The first figure and the X mean that the binocular magnifies 7 times; it would be called a 7-power binocular. The second figure indicates the diameter in millimeters of the objective lens of the binocular; this is the big lens nearest the object being viewed. The 7 x 35 binocular has an objective lens 35 millimeters in diameter.

Sometimes inferior makes of glasses have figures stamped on them that indicate a higher magnification than is actually provided. Magnification is easy to check, however. Focus your binocular on a small object about a hundred feet away. Look at the object through one barrel of the binocular only, leaving the other eye free to see the object without the aid of lenses. You will then see two images, the large one seen through the binocular and the smaller seen with the unaided eye. The number of times the large image is higher or wider than the small image is the actual magnifying power of the binocular.

WHAT IS RELATIVE BRIGHTNESS? In a binocular you want not only magnification, but also a bright, clear image. The relative brightness of one pair of binoculars to another is determined by the diameter of the objective lens in its relation to the magnification.

Divide the diameter of the objective lens by the magnification of the binocular and you get the diameter of what is called the *exit pupil*. Thus, the exit pupil of the 7 x 35 binocular is 5 millimeters in diameter. The exit pupil is the image of the objective lens formed by the eyepiece. You can see it by holding your glasses a foot or so away from you and against the sky. You will see a small circle of light in each eyepiece; this is the image of the objective opening in the lens that goes against the eye. It is the exit pupil.

This exit pupil indicates the diameter of the bundle of light that is offered to the eye. If the eye is to use all the light offered by the binocular, the diameter of the exit pupil should not be greater than the diameter of the pupil of the eye. The human eye contracts to approximately 2 millimeters in diameter in bright daylight and dilates to about 7 in complete darkness. Hence, binoculars for all-round daylight use are made with exit pupils ranging from 3 to 5 millimeters in diameter, because a bundle of light of this diameter will fill the human eye on the ordinary day. More light than this could not be used by the eye. So-called night glasses, the 7 x 50 or 6 x 42 models, have exit pupils of some 7 millimeters, and the completely dilated eye can use all the light they provide. Such glasses provide more light during the daytime than the eye can accommodate.

The *light value* or *relative brightness* of binoculars is the square of the diameter of the exit pupil. This relative-brightness factor is a handy way to compare one pair of binoculars with another. Most bird watchers prefer a relative brightness of at least 25. Hence, the 7 x 35 is a popular choice: divide the diameter of the objective lens, 35, by the magnification, 7, and you get 5 as the quotient: square this and you get 25 as the relative-brightness factor. In the West, where the air is clear and light more brilliant, binoculars like the 8 x 30 and 9 x 35, which have relative-brightness factors of approximately 15, may be used.

It is important to use all the light that a particular model of binoculars affords. That is why you should adjust the glasses so that the eye lines up exactly with the exit pupil in the binocular. The distance between the exit pupils is called *interpupillary distance.*

COATING OF LENSES. The brilliance of the image seen is affected not only by the size of the exit pupil but also by the light loss within the binocular. All glass surfaces reflect a certain fraction of light, and this applies to the glass surfaces in a binocular. There are usually ten of these, and if between 4 and 5 per cent of the light is lost at each surface, the aggregate loss is important. This loss can be reduced by approximately half if the glass surfaces are coated uniformly with a permanent low-reflecting film of vaporized metal salts or with other similar material. You can see this surfacing in the form of a purplish tint on the objective lens of the binocular, although the coating is actually colorless. Coating is a development that has come into practice largely since World War II.

The amount of light that is transmitted to the eye depends also upon the number of glass surfaces in the optical system of the binocular, the quality of glass used in making the lenses and prisms, and the skill of the lens grinders and polishers in making these optical parts.

WHY ALIGNMENT IS IMPORTANT. When a pair of binoculars is aligned perfectly, you see a single image with both eyes. Sometimes the prisms get out of position, or the frame becomes twisted so that you do not see just a single image. The eyes can compensate for this error to a certain extent, but eyestrain is likely to result. If you find that you suffer eyestrain after using binoculars, it is possible that the two barrels are not aligned perfectly. The remedy is to take them to a repairman.

The ability of the binocular to retain perfect alignment even under conditions of hard wear is one of the greatest mechanical differences between a fine binocular and one of inferior quality. The lenses and prisms of the latter may be manipulated initially to secure good alignment, but it may be destroyed by jars or bumps in service.

HOW TO FOCUS. There are two kinds of binoculars so far as method of focusing is concerned. One focuses by a central wheel. The other focuses by adjustments of the individual eyepieces. The central-focusing type is made with the right eyepiece adjustable to compensate for any visual differences between the eyes. This model is most popular, because it is easier to use. The individual focusing model is likely to be sturdier and more proof against moisture. It is preferred by the Army and Navy for this reason.

In either binocular, first swing the barrels on their hinges to adjust them to the proper distance between the eyes. This adjustment makes it possible for the images seen by the two eyes to be correctly superimposed, thus forming a single, clear picture.

Next, focus the eyepieces. If your binocular is of the central-focusing type, cover the objective lens which is on the same side as the adjustable eyepiece, and rotate the central focusing adjustment until the object seen is clear. Then cover the other objective lens, and turn the individual eyepiece adjustment until the object can be seen distinctly.

In using binoculars that have individual-eyepiece focusing, each eyepiece must be focused independently. It is harder, obviously, to adjust two eyepieces than it is to adjust a central focus, but a bit of practice will enable you to use such binoculars satisfactorily.

WHAT IS FIELD OF VIEW? "Field of view" is a term that describes the width of the view seen through a binocular at a given distance. This is the field of view in linear feet seen at 1,000 yards' distance. In the Galilean type of glass the field of view is limited by the size of the objective lens, and this, in turn, is limited by the distance between the eyes. In the prismatic binocular, the field of view is independent of the diameter of the objective lens; it is regulated, instead, by the type and design of the prisms and the eyepiece. You get a field of view only 60 yards in diameter when you look at an object 1,000 yards distant through a 6-power Galilean glass, but through the 6-power binocular you get a field of view almost 145 yards in diameter, or two and a half times as great; this gives you an area to inspect that is six times as great. A wide field of view makes it easier to locate objects and to keep pace with their motion. This is especially important in bird watching.

In testing the field of view of two binoculars of the same power, focus them on a landscape, and the one that shows the most widely separated objects in the landscape has the larger field.

In general, you see a larger area when you look through a binocular of low magnification than you do with one of high magnification. However, there is no way of knowing just what the field of view is without referring to the manufacturer's specifications. One of the best-known manufacturers in the United States has 8-power binoculars that have a wider field of view than his 7-power glasses, for instance.

Persons who wear eyeglasses cannot get their eyes close enough to the eyepiece (or ocular lens, as it is also called) to enjoy the full field of view that the binocular affords. However, they can buy flat eyecaps to screw on their binoculars in place of the regular deep eyecaps. This enables them to hold the binoculars closer to their eyes. These eyecaps cost only fifty cents each.

HOW MUCH SHOULD YOU PAY? One of the best makes of binoculars is a 7 x 35 glass that sells for $155.00, plus tax. This price includes leather case with straps. Those with less to spend can buy a serviceable glass for considerably less. Many Japanese glasses are being sold in this country, and they can be bought for $30.00 or less. It is obvious that neither the glass nor the mechanical parts can be of the quality of the $155.00 binocular, yet they have given real service to bird watchers, yachtsmen, and others I know who have used them. There is a chance here that the optical parts may get out of alignment easily; but if they are readjusted and fastened firmly in place, the glass may continue to give good service.

You can also buy good binoculars secondhand. I have a fine pair of German 10 x 50 war service glasses that I bought in a secondhand store for only $50.00. They would probably cost $200.00 new. My 20-power telescope is one of the finest made in this country, and cost $95.00 new.

WHAT ABOUT CLEANING? Don't try to take your binoculars apart to clean them yourself. To do so is to run the danger of putting the optical system out of alignment. There are from seventy to a hundred parts in a binocular, many of them requiring accurate adjustment. It is better to take your glasses to an optician or other expert who specializes in cleaning glasses. I recently had a pair of binoculars cleaned by a man in New York who spends all his time at such work. The job cost ten dollars, but it was worth it in the new satisfaction I was able to get from using the glasses. Finally, be careful about rubbing your glasses with cloth. Blow specks off first, as they may contain hard particles that will scratch the crystal if rubbed against the glass with a cloth.

You can keep rain off the ocular lenses of your binoculars when you are in the field by using a rain guard that is placed on the neck strap to slide up and down as needed. Price is approximately $2.50.

Reading references

Know Your Binoculars, by ROBERT J. and ELSA REICHERT, *Audubon Magazine,* Vol. 53, No. 1, January–February, 1951, pp. 45–50; Vol. 53, No. 2, March–April, 1951, pp. 105–109.

Binoculars and How to Choose Them, BAUSCH & LOMB OPTICAL COMPANY, Rochester, New York, 1951, 29 pp.

How to Select Binoculars, SQUARE D. COMPANY, Kollsman Instrument Division, Elmhurst, New York, 1947, 24 pp.

chapter 9 / Books about birds

Books used by bird watchers vary greatly according to individual preferences and interests, but I find that four basic books answer for me the four questions that are most important to bird watchers, namely, *What* is that bird? *Why* do birds do some of the things they do? *Where* can I find certain birds? *When* can I find certain birds in my neighborhood? This book tells *How*.

Four basic books

These basic books are as follows:

WHAT. *A Field Guide to the Birds*, by ROGER TORY PETERSON. This book tells how to identify birds. However, it is a guide for species found east of the Rockies, so that if you live in a Western state you would want to own Peterson's *A Field Guide to Western Birds*. RICHARD H. POUGH's *Audubon Bird Guide*, for Eastern birds, is another fine manual. His *Audubon Water Bird Guide* is a book that I always take on field trips, for its plates are excellent, and it gives more information about water birds and hawks than does Peterson.

WHY. *Birds of America*, edited by T. GILBERT PEARSON and others, tells much of the life histories of birds, and *why* and *how* they do certain things. Peterson identifies the birds, but Pearson's book tells about their interesting habits.

You may find that *Birds of America* does not quite suit you, because it is rather old and does not have quite so much information about each bird as you require. Then the thing to do is to consult ARTHUR CLEVELAND BENT's *Life Histories of North American Birds*. These books are rather hard to get now; they comprise 19 volumes that began to appear in 1919. However, libraries have them.

WHERE. *A Guide to Bird Finding East of the Mississippi*, by OLIN SEWALL PETTINGILL, JR., is the one I use. It tells what places in Eastern states are best for bird finding and what species you can find in each. If you live in a Western state you would rely upon PETTINGILL's *A Guide to Bird Finding West of the Mississippi*.

WHEN. *Birds around New York City*, by ALLAN D. CRUICKSHANK. This book tells me *when* to find all the species that occur in this large area around New York City, which is the region in which I live. It deals with relative frequency of occurrence and times of arrival and departure.

Of course, this book is of little use to you if you live outside the New York City region. However, there are many regional check lists and other documents that you can consult; there is something on the bird life of every state, ranging from the magnificent *Birds of Washington State* (767 pages), published in 1953 by the University of Washington Press, to such modest leaflets as *Common Land Birds of California* and *Water and Shore Birds of California*, published by the California Conservation Council in 1947.

Compact reference library

An excellent list of books for a small reference library has been compiled by Mrs. Monica de la Salle, librarian of the National Audubon Society in New York, and published in *Audubon Magazine* in March–April, 1952. She assumes that the bird watcher already owns a field guide or guides, and wants to supplement these books with a few volumes that will in a small space give as much information about birds as possible. She has six suggestions for books to satisfy three general purposes:

1. A good ornithological textbook, and a general reference work:
A Laboratory and Field Manual of Ornithology, by OLIN SEWALL PETTINGILL, JR.
A Dictionary of Birds, by ALFRED NEWTON *et al.*

2. A book on life histories of North American birds, illustrated in color, and a general book on bird habits and behavior:
Birds of America, edited by T. GILBERT PEARSON and others.
Birds and Their Attributes, by G. A. ALLEN.

3. One or two books for reading and for finding facts:
Birds over America, by ROGER TORY PETERSON.
This Fascinating Animal World, by ALAN DEVOE.

Mrs. de la Salle points out that these six books may be purchased for less than $30.00.

List of bird books

There follows a list of books about birds, divided into various classifications, as field guides, general reference works, and so on. By consulting this list, the bird watcher will be able to select volumes to meet his specific interest.

FIELD GUIDES. Field guides are handy books that you can carry in your pocket when you are out in the field. Their main function is to help you to identify birds.

A Field Guide to the Birds, by ROGER TORY PETERSON, Houghton Mifflin Company, Boston, 1947. Second revised and enlarged edition, 290 pp., plus 36 color plates, 22 plates in black and white. A popular guide to birds found east of the Rockies, with each species identified with text that describes field marks, voice, and range. In both text and picture the distinctive field marks are emphasized. End papers show silhouettes of birds.

Audubon Bird Guide, by RICHARD H. POUGH, Doubleday and Company, Inc., Garden City, New York, 1949, 312 pp., 48 color plates. There is little to choose between this and Peterson's guide; both have sold hundreds of thousands of copies.

Audubon Water Bird Guide, by RICHARD H. POUGH, Doubleday and Company, Inc., Garden City, New York, 1951, 352 pp. and 48 color plates and 100 line drawings. This is a good companion volume to either Peterson's guide or Pough's other volume. Text includes data on identification, measurements, habits, voice, nest, and range. Color plates are large enough to portray bird in detail. Birds of Eastern North America north of Mexico are included.

A Field Guide to Western Birds, by ROGER TORY PETERSON, Houghton Mifflin Company, Boston, 1941, 240 pp. and 5 color plates, 41 black-and-white plates, 40 text figures. This book lacks the many color plates found in the guide to Eastern birds. It covers the area roughly from the Pacific through the Rockies to the western parts of the Great Plains.

How to Know the Birds, by ROGER TORY PETERSON, The New American Library, New York. Line drawings and silhouettes of more than 200 species. 35 cents.

Pocket Guide to the Birds, by ALLAN D. CRUICKSHANK, Dodd, Mead & Company, New York, 1953, 216 pp., 72 natural-color illustrations and 78 drawings. Includes birds of Eastern and Central North America.

Birds, by H. S. ZIM and A. C. MARTIN, illustrated by Rudolph Freund, Simon and Schuster, New York, 1949. A handy dollar book that identifies 265 species, contains 112 full-color plates, 128 silhouettes, range maps.

Field Guide to Birds of the West Indies, by JAMES BOND, The Macmillan Company, New York, 1947, 257 pp., 211 line drawings and one color plate.

Birds of Mexico, by EMMET REID BLAKE, The University of Chicago Press, Chicago, 1953, 644 pp. and drawings.

A Pocket Guide to British Birds, by R. S. R. FITTER and R. A. RICHARDSON, Dodd, Mead and Company, New York, 1953, 240 pp., 1,000 illustrations, with 600 in color.

A Field Guide to the Birds of Britain and Europe, by ROGER TORY PETERSON, GUY MOUNTFORT, and P. A. D. HOLLOM, Houghton Mifflin Company, Boston, 1954, 318 pp., 1,107 illustrations and 367 maps.

GENERAL REFERENCE BOOKS. These are books that contain more information about a bird's behavior or habits than can usually be found in the field guides. All except Chapman's are liberally illustrated.

Birds of America, edited by T. GILBERT PEARSON with John Burroughs as consulting editor and six assisting editors, Garden City Publishing Company, Inc., Garden City, New York, 1936, 832 pp., and 106 color plates by Louis Agassiz Fuertes. Although this book was first published in 1917, it is an excellent work of reference and is available in bookstores at a price that is modest for such a handsome volume. The text descriptions of birds are very detailed, and the text about habits and food is excellent.

Handbook of Birds of Eastern North America, by FRANK M. CHAPMAN, D. Appleton–Century Co., New York, 1934, 2nd rev. ed., 581 pp., 29 plates, 166 text figures. This book was first published in 1895, and was the standard book for identification until Peterson and Pough. There are few color plates, but there is valuable introductory material of 133 pages that includes a historical review of bird watching (1895–1911), paragraphs about finding and naming birds, and the study of birds in reference to distribution, migration, voice, nesting, plumage, food, and general characteristics.

Land Birds of America, by ROBERT CUSHMAN MURPHY and DEAN AMADON, McGraw-Hill Book Company, Inc., New York, 1953, 240 pp., and 221 color plates of photographs and 15 in black and white. This book justifies the publisher's claim of being the greatest contribution to picturing birds in their natural habitat since the works of Audubon. Full-length commentaries by Dr.

Murphy and Dr. Amadon run to 55,000 words and cover physical characteristics, range, and habits.

Birds of Middle and North America, by ROBERT RIDGWAY, Smithsonian Institution, Government Printing Office, Washington, D.C., 1901–19, 10 vols. This is one of the classics of American ornithology, written by a man who was curator of birds in the U.S. National Museum for more than 50 years.

The Book of Birds, edited by GILBERT GROSVENOR, ALEXANDER WETMORE, *et al.*, National Geographic Society, Washington, D.C., 1937, Vol. 1, 357 pp., Vol. 2, 374 pp., 204 color plates, 228 black-and-white photographs. These two volumes bring together the articles on birds that have been written for *National Geographic Magazine* over the years. There are brief biographies of 633 species, showing size, range, and behavior, and listing subspecies. Some 500 species are illustrated in color, mainly by Allan Brooks.

The Birds of America, by JOHN JAMES AUDUBON, The Macmillan Company, New York, 1946, 435 color plates on 218 leaves. This famous work was first published in this edition in 1937 with 500 plates; the 1946 printing is the fifth.

The Ducks, Geese and Swans of North America, by FRANCIS H. KORTRIGHT, American Wildlife Institute, Washington, D.C., 1942, 476 pp., 36 color plates, 159 drawings in black and white. The illustrations are splendid and show eclipse plumage.

Birds of the Ocean, by W. B. ALEXANDER, G. P. Putnam's Sons, New York, 1928, 428 pp. Although illustrated only in black and white, it is one of the best guides to gulls, shearwaters, petrels, tropic birds, and other birds of the ocean.

The Handbook of British Birds, by H. F. WITHERBY, F. C. R. JOURDAIN, N. F. TICEHURST, and B. W. TUCKER; H. F. & G. Witherby, Ltd., London, 1938, 5 vols. This is the best general reference work on the birds of western Europe, giving complete data on each species.

WHERE TO FIND BIRDS. In addition to owning a book that helps the bird watcher to identify the birds that he finds, he needs a book to tell him where to go. Two books by Olin Sewall Pettingill, Jr., supply this need.

A Guide to Bird Finding East of the Mississippi, by OLIN
SEWALL PETTINGILL, JR., Oxford University Press, New York,
1951, 659 pp. This book, which contains numerous line sketches
of birds by George Miksch Sutton, is divided into chapters according to states. Each state's best birding areas are listed alphabetically. There is an introduction to each chapter which describes the state's physiographic regions (e.g., coastal plains,
mountain systems) or biological communities (e.g., coniferous
forests, prairie grasslands) and the general nature of the bird life
to be found in each. The book contains specific instructions on
how to get to the places listed and mentions the birds that will be
found in each place. This volume covers the twenty-six states
lying entirely east of the Mississippi River.

A Guide to Bird Finding West of the Mississippi, by OLIN
SEWALL PETTINGILL, JR., Oxford University Press, New York,
1953, 709 pp. This book is also illustrated with incidental line
drawings of birds by George Miksch Sutton. This volume is a
counterpart of *A Guide to Bird Finding East of the Mississippi*,
and is identical with it in organization and style. Twenty-two
western states are covered.

LIFE HISTORIES. American ornithologists are producing an increasing number of detailed life histories of birds, a good example
of which is *Studies in the Life History of the Song Sparrow*, by
MARGARET M. NICE. However, the comprehensive work is *Life
Histories of North American Birds*, by ARTHUR CLEVELAND BENT,
United States National Museum, Washington, D.C. Mr. Bent's
great cooperative enterprise was begun in 1919, and by 1953 he
had completed nineteen volumes. These volumes could be procured, when published, from the United States Government
Printing Office for prices ranging from 50 cents to $4.50. How-
ever, the supply of each was soon exhausted, so that now they
must be obtained in secondhand bookstores. There are sets in
some libraries and individual volumes in others. (Dover Publications has undertaken to put out reprints of Bent and has issued
a few volumes. Text is practically as in the original, but there are
fewer illustrations.) The text of these books is easy to read, and
there are many photographs. The volumes summarize what is
known about all the species and subspecies of birds found in North

America. The nineteen volumes are as follows, the figure preceding each being the United States National Museum bulletin number:

107. *Life Histories of North American Diving Birds*, 1919.
113. *Life Histories of North American Gulls and Terns*, 1921.
121. *Life Histories of North American Petrels, Pelicans, and Their Allies*, 1922.
126. *Life Histories of North American Wild Fowl*, Part 1, 1923.
130. *Life Histories of North American Wild Fowl*, Part 2, 1925.
135. *Life Histories of North American Marsh Birds*, 1926.
142. *Life Histories of North American Shore Birds*, Part 1, 1927.
146. *Life Histories of North American Shore Birds*, Part 2, 1929.
162. *Life Histories of North American Gallinaceous Birds*, 1932.
167. *Life Histories of North American Birds of Prey*, Part 1, 1937.
170. *Life Histories of North American Birds of Prey*, Part 2, 1938.
174. *Life Histories of North American Woodpeckers*, 1939.
176. *Life Histories of North American Cuckoos, Goatsuckers, Hummingbirds and Their Allies*, 1940.
179. *Life Histories of North American Flycatchers, Larks, Swallows, and Their Allies*, 1942.
191. *Life Histories of North American Jays, Crows, and Titmice*, 1947.
195. *Life Histories of North American Nuthatches, Wrens, Thrashers, and Their Allies*, 1948.
196. *Life Histories of North American Thrushes, Kinglets, and Their Allies*, 1949.
197. *Life Histories of North American Wagtails, Shrikes, Vireos, and Their Allies*, 1950.
203. *Life Histories of North American Wood Warblers*, 1953.

REGIONAL STUDIES. Every bird student will want to consult studies of his own region, state, county, or community. Such studies will tell him what birds he may expect to find in these areas, and often they give data about the relative abundance of the bird, dates of arrival and departure for migrants, and dates when eggs have been found. There are so many of these studies that it would be impossible to list even the more outstanding here. One of the most imposing is *Birds of Washington State*, by STAN-

LEY G. JEWETT, WALTER P. TAYLOR, WILLIAM T. SHAW, and JOHN W. ALDRICH, the University of Washington Press, Seattle, 1953, 767 pp. and 12 color plates, 99 halftones, 50 distribution maps, and a colored life-zone map. I have mentioned that I have found ALLAN D. CRUICKSHANK's *Birds around New York City* of much use. Some other new and excellent studies are as follows:

Florida Bird Life, by ALEXANDER SPRUNT, JR., Coward-McCann, New York, 1954, 576 pp., 40 full-page color plates, 65 black-and-white maps.

An Album of Southern Birds, photographs by SAMUEL A. GRIMES and text by ALEXANDER SPRUNT, JR., University of Texas Press, Austin, Texas, 103 pp., 4 color plates and monochrome plates.

Arizona and Its Bird Life, by HERBERT BRANDT, Bird Research Foundation, Cleveland, 1951, 723 pp., illus., part color, map.

The Birds of New Brunswick, by W. AUSTIN SQUIRES, Monographic Series No. 4, The New Brunswick Museum, St. John, N.B., 1952, 164 pp., illustrations.

About the best regional study is *The Birds of Massachusetts and Other New England States,* by EDWARD HOWE FORBUSH, Massachusetts Department of Agriculture, Boston, 1925–29, 3 vols. This work, beautifully illustrated by Louis Agassiz Fuertes and Allan Brooks, gives popularly written and quite detailed life accounts.

A large collection of pamphlets on local bird life is in the files of the National Audubon Society, 1130 Fifth Avenue, New York, and an inquiry there will elicit information about what is available on a specific area. The Society also has a substantial collection of bound volumes that are local studies.

I suggest that the student get in touch with his local library or state department of agriculture or conservation for information as to available studies or lists. Sometimes these state departments have themselves produced worth-while documents. Mention has been made of the check lists of California birds published by the California Conservation Council in Santa Barbara. The State Department of History and Archives of Iowa also published in 1953 a supplement to an earlier check list of Iowa birds.

Finally, and importantly, do not overlook *Audubon Field Notes,* published by the National Audubon Society in collaboration with the United States Fish and Wildlife Service. This is a bimonthly magazine devoted to reporting the distribution, migration, and abundance of birds all over the country. Subscription price is $3.00 a year.

BOOKS ON BIRD STUDY. Other books on bird watching are largely British, as the art is older and more widespread in that country. There is one good American book, by Hickey, designed for rather advanced students.

A Guide to Bird Watching, by JOSEPH J. HICKEY, Oxford University Press, New York, 1943, 264 pp. Illustrations by Francis Lee Jaques and bird tracks by Charles A. Urner. This book contains chapters on how to begin bird study, the lure of migration watching, adventures in bird counting, explorations in bird distribution, the romance of bird banding, and the art of bird watching. There are 28 tables showing some of the examples and results of bird watching.

Watching Birds, by JAMES FISHER, Penguin Books, Inc., London, rev. ed., 1951, 188 pp. This inexpensive book for British bird watchers has chapters on the tools of bird watching, migration, where birds live, the numbers of birds, how birds recognize one another, territorial rights, and other subjects.

How to Study Birds, by STUART SMITH, Collins, London, 1947, 192 pp., with photographs. Another book for British bird watchers, but of interest to Americans, this volume is designed to interest bird watchers in the aspects of bird behavior rather than in the search for rarities and the compilation of lists of birds. Written in a simple style, it attempts to suggest to the average bird watcher new angles of approach to his hobby.

OTHER BOOKS. There follow various references on subjects such as attracting birds, bird songs, photography, migration, and so on that may be helpful to bird watchers who have special interests they wish to pursue:

A Guide to Bird Songs, by ARETAS A. SAUNDERS, Doubleday and Company, Inc., Garden City, New York, 1951, 307 pp. and diagrams. Descriptions and diagrams according to an ingenious system worked out by the author of the songs and singing habits of 108 land birds of the northeastern states.

American Bird Songs, recorded by ALBERT R. BRAND BIRD SONG FOUNDATION, Laboratory of Ornithology, Cornell University, Comstock Publishing Company, Ithaca, N.Y., 1942, six double-disk records.

Bird-Ringing, by R. M. LOCKLEY and ROSEMARY RUSSELL; Crosby, Lockwood & Son, Ltd., London, 1953, photographs and line drawings. There is no American book on the subject of bird banding.

Wings at My Window, by ADA CLAPHAM GOVAN, The Macmillan Company, New York, 1947, 197 pp. The fabulously successful story of a fabulously successful back-yard sanctuary.

Songbirds in Your Garden, by JOHN K. TERRES, Thomas Y. Crowell Co., New York, 1953, 274 pp. This book, written by the managing editor of *Audubon Magazine,* tells about feeding birds to attract them, birdhouses, offering water, care and feeding of young birds, ornamental plantings, making sounds to attract birds.

Photography Afield, by ORMAL I. SPRUNGMAN, The Stackpole Company, Harrisburg, Pennsylvania, 1951, 449 pp. and illustrations.

The Migration of Birds, by FREDERICK C. LINCOLN, Fish and Wildlife Service, U.S. Department of the Interior, Washington, D.C., 1950, 102 pp., Circular No. 16. This is a condensation of the author's *The Migration of American Birds,* first published in 1939.

Feathered Wings, by ANTHONY JACK, Methuen & Co., Ltd., London, 1953, 131 pp. and 15 photographic plates and diagrams.

Wildlife Conservation, by IRA N. GABRIELSON, The Macmillan Company, New York, 1941, 250 pp. A discussion of the many problems connected with conservation.

Birds' Nests, by RICHARD HEADSTROM, Ives Washburn, Inc., New York, 1949, 128 pp. and 61 photographs of nests and birds.

Birds' Nests of the West, by RICHARD HEADSTROM, Ives Washburn, Inc., New York, 1951, 177 pp. and 32 photographs.

chapter 10 / Should you keep records?

A bird watcher can enjoy birds without keeping records, but he may enjoy them more if he does. However, the matter of records is relatively simple.

NOTEBOOK. I advocate that every bird watcher take afield with him a notebook and a stubby pencil. The pencil will fit easily into any pocket. I suggest that the notebook be of loose-leaf construction, with ruled pages 3 by 5 inches. I have tried other kinds of books, and find this the best. The book comes with a black imitation-leather cover, and additional pages can be bought in the five-and-ten-cent store.

The advantage of a loose-leaf notebook is that the leaves can be taken out and filed. If you are in the field and see a bird whose identity puzzles you, then is the time to make notes in your book, so that when you get home you can more readily find the name of the bird in question. You can file the page with other data on that bird, or transfer the note to other permanent records and destroy the loose-leaf page.

There are lots of other uses for such a book. You can jot down the expense of field trips, including your gasoline and oil, meals, and other expenditures. You can write down the names of other bird watchers you meet or those who accompany you, so that you can later refer to them for any necessary corroboration of bird discovery. You can note other natural phenomena of the season, the first flowers, the insects that are about, the names of the early butterflies, the dates when you heard the first peepers. In making notes about birds use ♂ for male and ♀ for female. Note the number or approximate number of individuals of a species you see in any day, and details about place, weather, and date. Such a book may be kept as a diary. Use it also to note the exposures and times on photographs you take.

These loose-leaf pages are the size of an ordinary 3- by 5-inch index card; hence they can be filed readily in the same file with index cards that you may use for other purposes.

Such pages, if kept carefully, serve many purposes. One of the advantages of records is that, if kept chronologically, they serve to remind you each year of aspects of nature for which you should be alert. Half of the success of bird watching consists in knowing what to expect. If you look at your loose-leaf file to see what you found afield on the third of April last year, and note that killdeer were abundant, you are alert for this bird when you go afield, and are therefore more likely to see it.

CHECK LISTS. Bird check lists can be obtained from a variety of sources. They are printed lists, about 4 by 6 or 7 inches, and list in A.O.U.* order the birds that you are likely to find in your part of the country. These cards may be obtained from the National Audubon Society or from local groups. The New Jersey Audubon Society has its own check list, for instance, which it sells to members for five cents each. These lists give the names of birds, so that you merely have to make a check opposite the

* American Ornithologists' Union.

species you see, and note how many individuals of each species, and they also provide spaces for indicating who went on the trip with you, what the temperature was, and where you went.

The advantage of keeping such lists is that they give you good records of each field trip. You do not have to do any writing, but merely make a mark opposite the name of each new bird you see. At the bottom of the lists there is a space to indicate the total number of species seen. The A.O.U. order is not alphabetical, but lists the birds in the order of their development, with the loons and grebes first and the finches last. Once you get used to it, this order is relatively easy to follow.

These cards can also be filed conveniently. If there is any question of what bird you saw on any trip or how many birds or who was with you, all you have to do is to look in your file of these check lists and you will find the information readily available.

LIFE LISTS. I keep my *life list*, that is, the birds I have seen during my whole life, on larger cards. These cards are 4 by 6 inches, and ruled. This is a standard size for an index card. I use this larger card because you can get more information on it, and you need more information in such a life list. I have one card for each bird, and typewrite on the card the name of the bird, the time and circumstances under which I saw it first, and who was with me at the time. Then I indicate on the same card the subsequent times that I have seen the bird and the circumstances.

You have to use discretion in maintaining such a record. You would not write down each time you saw a blue jay, but you might indicate each time you saw a long-billed curlew. In connection with the more common birds, it is worth while to indicate the more uncommon circumstances under which you see them. You may have some interesting note about blue jays nesting, as I did one year when jays nested in our rose arbor, and I found the nestlings on the ground dead, one after another. That is something you may wish to put on your big card.

It is a good idea to indicate who else was on your trip with you, for various reasons. Some question about the identification of the bird might come up, and you would want to know who might be consulted in substantiation. I know, for instance, who was with me the first time I saw a long-billed curlew. Moreover, if you have children, and take them along, and they see the same birds that you see, as they probably do, then it may be of interest to them in later years to be able to compile life lists of their own on the basis of information that you have kept so carefully.

It is of interest to my wife and me to look at Roger Tory Peterson's life list in the front of his *Field Guide to the Birds*. We check against his list the birds we have seen, and take pleasure in approaching his total.

Any time you think you have compiled a long life list, think of Ludlow Griscom, Harvard's noted ornithologist. His life list includes 2,500 birds, which he has seen in many lands. There are 720 species of birds in the United States, and anyone who has seen 300 of them has done extraordinarily well. This does not include subspecies, of which there are approximately as many as there are species.

The National Audubon Society sells cards that can be used to keep life lists.

DIARY. There is no need to keep another diary if you keep notes on your life lists about your different species, and keep in your card index the 3- by 5-inch pages from your loose-leaf notebook. However, some people do like a more formal bound journal or diary, and for this purpose any book of somewhat standard letter-page size, that is, 8 by 10 or 8½ by 11 inches, should suffice. I kept such a diary when I was a boy; it does induce you to put down thoughts that you would not be likely to record if you were writing on a smaller page. Sometimes these reflections are a most valuable part of your bird-watching activity. My experience is that such books, although bravely started, are seldom carried forward with persistence. In a life that is complicated enough, it is not desirable to complicate it further with unnecessary records, unless one has the time for such things and has some definite purpose in mind.

FILES. I maintain three kinds of files. One is a wooden file for 3- by 5-inch loose-leaf pages and cards of the same size. The other is a larger file for 4- by 6-inch cards and for check lists of field trips. The third file is for clippings. I had it made especially for me by a stationer. It is 18 inches long by 10 inches wide by

8 inches high. It is heavy cardboard, covered with black fabric, and of the pull-drawer type. I have them made one at a time, and they cost $4.80 each. I now have twelve, and pile them on a table so that they are three files high and four abreast. I file my clippings in these files, and merely order more files as my clippings expand. Of course, I have the ordinary steel cabinets for filing letter-size folders, but I use them for business other than birds.

CLIPPINGS. After many years of experimenting with the filing of clippings, I have developed the following system. As I clip items from newspapers or magazines, I mark on the item the date and source. Sometimes I paste these clippings on half of a standard piece of letter-size paper, an 8- by 10- or 8½- by 11-inch page. I find these half sheets easy to handle. A larger size would be too big for most clippings, while a smaller size would not be big enough. These pages fit in the black-fabric-covered files I have mentioned. They are filed according to subject; that is, all birds are filed together, alphabetically by the bird, all trees are filed together, all flowers, and so on. I do not always paste the clippings on half pages, although I did so for many years. I now have envelopes approximately the size of these half sheets, that are open on the long side. I merely put the clippings in these envelopes, and mark the subject on the envelope. This is the way clippings are kept in some newspaper files or "morgues."

I started my file of clippings some forty years ago when I was a boy, and for years it was maintained by my invalid mother, who took a great interest in it. She went through papers and magazines for me religiously every day, clipping and filing. I owe a vast debt of gratitude to her for this work, for it has greatly helped me in my writing on nature subjects. There must be twenty thousand or more clippings in this file by now, and hardly a subject appears in the daily papers on any phase of nature upon which I cannot produce a handful of clippings.

Of course, not many would want to keep such an extensive file. But everyone does want to keep certain clippings, and if he does he should keep them in an orderly way. It is almost useless to keep them in a scrapbook where they are pasted on pages, as no order is possible in such a system and it is unwieldy and generally inefficient.

The only scrapbook or book of clippings that I keep is of my column in the *Newark News*. I keep these pasted, one to a page, in loose-leaf binders that have heavy scrapbook paper and an over-all size of 10 by 12 inches. I have been writing these columns weekly since February, 1947, so I have four books filled by now. Since they are all arranged in chronological order, it is easy to find what I want. It is especially easy because all the subjects treated have been indexed on 3- by 5-inch cards and filed in the card file of that size. If I want to know whether I have written on any subject at any time, I merely have to look at my 3- by 5-inch card index and find the date, and then refer to my column scrapbook to see the reference.

SKETCHES OR DRAWINGS. Persons so gifted can make sketches that they may wish to keep for artistic or scientific recollection. Even those who possess only the drawing talent required in a laboratory course in zoology or botany may make effective sketches of birds or parts of birds for use in identification. If these are made on a card 3 by 5 or 4 by 6 inches, they can be filed with other cards of the same size. If they are made on larger paper, other systems may have to be devised.

PHOTOGRAPHS. A photographic record is incomparable, of course, whether of black-and-white prints or color transparencies. The subject of bird photography will be discussed in a chapter of its own. Here again I advocate a card filing system for keeping the prints, rather than bulky albums. Obviously each print should be identified as to subject, where and when taken, and the time, exposure, and kind of camera used.

chapter 11 / Fun on field trips

There are all kinds of field trips. There are the casual walks you take in your local park, the visit to a marsh or reservoir a few miles distant, the all-day trip with your bird club to watch migrating shore birds, or the more difficult operation that entails traveling hundreds of miles to observe the bird life of an unfamiliar area. You will make some of these trips by yourself, others with your family or with groups of bird watchers. I enjoy all these kinds of trips, and in this chapter will describe some I have taken and the birds I have seen.

When I was a boy I did most of my bird watching alone, but since I have been married my wife has been my companion. Some bird watchers prefer to travel alone. Their point of view is stated by Edward Howe Forbush, distinguished author of *The Birds of Massachusetts and Other New England States:* *

"When one is in the company of others, nature never completely enthralls him. His attention is more or less distracted by his companions; he fails to see and hear all. The bird student should attend entirely to the birds, and then they will requite his singleness of purpose. When alone, he has no one to talk to, and no interruptions. The human voice warns all creatures from afar of the approach of their arch enemy, man; let it be stilled, and nature is at peace."

This is a rather severe attitude; most bird watchers do not have the great singleness of purpose of Mr. Forbush, or else find that the advantages of companionship more than offset the disadvantages. Two pairs of eyes and ears can catch more than one pair, and the aggregate experience of a group can be brought to bear upon knotty problems of bird finding and identification. Perhaps an extreme case of the advantage of a group is in the annual Christmas bird census, when from ten to forty persons or more cooperate in thorough tallies of species in restricted areas. True, it is somewhat unprofitable for the experienced bird watcher to be thrown in with a band of children or with a large number of adults, perhaps a hundred or more, who are largely beginners and not equipped either with experience or proper glasses. The children may have a tendency to be noisy and overactive, while the aggregation of adults is unwieldy. However, these are opportunities for the veteran bird watcher to share with others the superior knowledge he enjoys.

Field trips in spring

Spring is the most exciting time for bird walks, chiefly because of the waves of warblers that may be seen and because the experience of finding the first birds of the year is accompanied by discovery of the first flowers.

* Edward Howe Forbush, "Out-door Bird Study," section in *Birds of America,* edited by T. Gilbert Pearson *et al.,* Garden City Publishing Company, Inc., Garden City, N.Y., 1936, p. xxv.

MAY IN THE SWAMP. Every May, generally on a day from the tenth to the fifteenth, my wife and I lead a group of bird watchers through Hatfield Swamp. This is a large area of fresh-water marsh not far from my home. It is an area that surrounds the confluence of the Passaic, Rockaway, and Whippany Rivers, and holds marshy meadows, thick woods, both deciduous and evergreen, and heavy undergrowth. The swamp is traversed in one direction by an elevated boardwalk that runs under electric-power transmission lines, and in another direction by a wagon road that is drier than the surrounding area.

On one occasion we found a blue-gray gnatcatcher's nest, with the birds flying excitedly around it. The nest had been built at the juncture of a small tree with one of its branches, and the nest covering matched the bark so closely that it would not have been noticed had not the birds been seen to fly to it. There is only one other breeding record for our region, a nest found in May, 1928. The bird itself is unusual in this area, not more than a dozen individuals being seen in it in any one year. We saw a female cowbird lurking nearby, and hoped this unhappy parasite was not successful in laying one of its own eggs in the nest of the gnatcatcher.

Warblers were plentiful, and in one group of trees we counted seven species at one time, the magnolia, parula, black-and-white, black-poll, chestnut-sided, black-throated green, and myrtle warblers. Other species in the swamp were the Blackburnian, bay-breasted, and Wilson's warblers.

These gems of the bird world had competition for interest, however. The yellow-throated and white-eyed vireos were numerous, visible, and vocal. In one field a pair of bobolinks flew low over the dandelions and golden ragwort, singing their ebullient songs and displaying their handsome black-and-white coats. A pair of solitary sandpipers stood like sentinels on the sandy shore of a brook tributary to the Passaic River, nodding solemnly every now and then, as is their habit.

At another place a purple martin flew overhead and an American bittern arose from the marsh. A scarlet tanager alighted in a tree directly over us, and a northern water thrush flew noisily from a rivulet beside the boardwalk.

BIG DAY IN MAY. One of the ornithological customs in these parts is the Big Day, which is pursued most vigorously by members of the Urner Ornithological Club. This group of able birders is named after Charles A. Urner, who is reputed to have instituted the practice of spending many hours afield on one promising day in May, to try to compile a large list of species noted. One recent Big Day the members of the Urner Club saw 175 different species in a twenty-four-hour marathon that covered 425 miles. There were sixteen observers in four automobiles, and they explored likely areas in Boonton, Troy Meadows, Bound Brook, Barnegat, Beach Haven Inlet, and other places. Among the interesting birds noted were an American eagle at Boonton Reservoir, a summer tanager at Barnegat Light, black rails and oystercatchers at Beach Haven, and a thousand brant at Tuckerton. All three of the latter places are on the Jersey shore.

FIRST ARMY BIRD WALK. One of the most unusual bird walks I ever led was on a May morning when I took eighty-one persons, all officers of the First Army and their families, on a trip to New York City's Central Park. We left at six o'clock in the morning from Governor's Island, by ferry and by bus. A close friend of mine was the ordnance officer and a former schoolmate the provost marshal; the former arranged for everyone to be equipped with Army binoculars, and the latter provided an escort of military police.

The morning was dull and wet, so we made no records, finding 20 species. Highlights were a blue-gray gnatcatcher and a nesting mallard. I took along two of the large charts produced by the National Audubon Society, and before we left the park pointed out the birds we had seen and told a little about each. The expedition was helpful in introducing the children to rather common species of birds, and in kindling an interest that might lead to their eventual broadening of this acquaintance. Most of the children were Scouts, Cubs, or Brownies.

Central Park is normally a good place to find birds in the spring. Northbound flights stop there for rest and food, and it is possible to count 78 species of migrants in a day. The park is favored because it is an oasis of green in a desert of cement. Moreover, migrating birds that fly by night are attracted by the city's lights.

One can find approximately 130 species of birds in the park in the course of a year. The most popular area is the Ramble, between 72nd and 79th Streets, while the haunt of marsh birds is near the 86th Street reservoir.

BULL'S ISLAND. For birds, give me the barrier beaches. Plum Island, Island Beach, Long Beach, Galveston Island, and Bull's Island, but of them all, the richest in bird life is the last. It is some fifteen miles north of Charleston, and is part of the Cape Romain National Wildlife Refuge. It is an island of 5,000 acres, ideal for birds because of dense, semitropical vegetation, its sea beach, salt marshes, fresh-water ponds, and strategic position on the Atlantic flyway. I visited the island in early spring one year when Mr. and Mrs. Joseph Moffitt still maintained the inn there for bird watchers and fishermen. Since then they have given up this occupation, and at the present writing there are no overnight accommodations, and no easy way to get to Bull's Island itself.

There is a half-hour's motorboat trip from the mainland to the island, and on the way I saw eight oyster-catchers standing on the edge of the marsh or flying low over the water with a display of white wing patterns, dark head, and large red bill. The bird is almost 20 inches from bill to tail.

Practically the entire oyster-catcher population of the Atlantic coast congregates in this refuge during the winter. This spectacular bird has been persecuted so severely that it is now absent from many parts of our coast. A few of the birds are found off the Jersey coast near Tuckerton. The oyster-catcher feeds on oysters, clams, snails, and other creatures found on the wilder outer beaches. It is expert at capturing shellfish by inserting its bill into the partly open shell and cutting the muscle before the bivalve can close its shell again.

Various bird watchers who have visited Bull's Island over the years have compiled a list of some 230 species of birds observed there. Included are many birds that hardly ever visit the more northern latitudes. I saw some of these species—the ground dove, red-bellied woodpecker, black vulture, boat-tailed grackle, and white-eyed towhee. The dove is similar to the mourning dove, but not much larger than a sparrow. The red-bellied woodpecker is smaller than a flicker, and the male has a red cap and striped back.

I also saw marbled godwits, Caspian tern, blue-gray gnatcatchers, pileated woodpeckers, willets, and many other notable species. Wild turkeys are on the island, and wood ibis, Wayne's clapper rails, white ibis, and long-billed curlews are other species to be encountered. When I visited the island, in March, it was too early to see the painted buntings, most gaily colored of American species.

The vegetation of the island is dense, marked by palmettos, live oaks, hanging Spanish moss, wild bamboo, and many vines. I might add that it rained heavily all the time I was on the island, otherwise I would have seen many more birds. It was impossible to keep binoculars dry in the torrents that came down.

Summer bird watching

Summer is the time to observe birds while they are rearing their families. Early-morning walks in June are also inspiring because of the great chorus of bird song. As summer wanes the birds begin to drift south, and in late August the migration of shore birds and terns becomes exciting.

CAPE COD IN THE SUMMER. Anyone who passes a summer vacation in an area other than his own may have an opportunity to observe a somewhat different bird life. For many years I have spent holidays on Cape Cod, at Wellfleet, near the tip of the Cape, or at Chatham, at the elbow, or at Bourne, where the Canal joins Buzzard's Bay.

At Wellfleet you are on a strip of land that is barely two miles wide, extending from the ocean to Massachusetts Bay. I like to set up my telescope on the headlands on the ocean side. These range from 50 to 100 feet in height, and I can look far out to sea. Thus I see oceanic birds that I would never see ordinarily, even with my 10-power binoculars. One day, for instance, I noticed two to three miles at sea some rather large birds that were gliding over the waves on stiffly extended wings, tipping to one side or the other as if trimming sail. This was the sooty shearwater, which in profile reminds you somewhat of a chimney swift. It is sooty, as is the swift, and has the same long, narrow wings and stubby tail. But there the resemblance ends, for the shearwater has a wingspread of some 40 inches, and a length of 18. It lives on squids and small fish, and, like the petrel, it builds its nest in an underground chamber at the end of a 2- to 3-foot burrow.

I also saw many Wilson's petrels from the headlands farther down the beach at Nauset. The petrels were numerous, whereas the shearwaters flew in twos and threes. The Wilson's petrel is the bird that is also named stormy petrel or Mother Carey's chicken. It is sometimes called sea swallow, which is an accurate name, for the bird is like a swallow in its flight and approximately the same size. The petrels I saw had a square tail; the Leach's petrel has a forked tail, more like that of a tree swallow or a purple martin. Both birds are sooty brown, with white rumps. I had seen the Wilson's petrel in the Gulf of St. Lawrence the previous summer.

Fall migration

More birds are about in September than in any other month, although they are not so noticeable as in the spring because of the heavy foliage. In my region the two most interesting aspects of the fall migration are the flights of the hawks along the mountain ridges and the migration of the shore birds.

VISIT TO CAPE MAY. I always go to Cape May in September or October, generally with the New Jersey Audubon Society, which has an annual field trip there. There are few people other than bird watchers in this resort in these months, but there are many birds there. We make our headquarters in one of the hotels that remain open for this occasion, and it is pleasant to eat and otherwise associate together. On my last trip there were some 500 persons, who had come from all counties of the state to witness the fascinating passage of the flocks.

Cape May Point is approximately the latitude of Washington. It is the tip of a funnel in which migrating birds are trapped by the ocean on one side and Delaware Bay on the other. They rest there briefly before attempting the hop across the bay.

Bird life at Cape May is fascinating not only because of the great flocks that congregate there, but also because of the numerous species represented and the occasional rarities included. We saw some 120 different species over the week end, with spectacular numbers of myrtle warblers, blue jays, Canada geese, American scoters, palm warblers, black skimmers, and meadowlarks. Among these flocks were several unusual birds. I saw four stilt sandpipers in a duck pond, a half dozen white-crowned sparrows, at both this place and Lily Lake, and four yellow-crowned night herons at Stone Harbor on the ocean side. Others saw a clay-colored sparrow, and one man found three dickcissels behind the very hotel where we were staying.

There were disappointments, too. The glossy ibises that had frequented Lighthouse Pond had left for the South, and the six African cattle egrets that had lived on a nearby farm all summer had likewise disappeared, although I saw them in a subsequent year.

The week end included a visit to the heronry at Stone Harbor, one of the few unspoiled dune areas with their native thickets and woods that are left along the barrier islands. We counted the birds that came to roost after a day of foraging in the marshes, and then tallied the night herons that at the same sunset hour left for their nocturnal feeding grounds.

I had never realized before this trip the extent of the migration of blue jays. I know that they move around a great deal in the fall, and some winters they seem to be almost lacking. However, there are usually a good number around all year. On this week end, however, and in some four hours of observation, I counted approximately a thousand blue jays in high flocks that were coming in from the sea. They had apparently passed land's end and decided to turn back. In fact, next to myrtle warblers, they were the most numerous species. However, there seems little evidence that this kind of migration depletes our winter population very seriously. The nearby Summit Nature Club makes annual winter censuses, and has counted between 250 and 500 blue jays each winter for the last five tallies. This is approximately the same number as the white-throated sparrows and black-capped chickadees observed.

HAWKS IN SEPTEMBER. September is the month to watch hawks migrate along the ridges, although their migration continues into

November. It is a pleasant occupation on a day around the third week end in September to climb to some sunny height and lie there in the beneficent warmth while the great birds sail overhead.

Hawks are strong-winged birds, but they like to fly low in migration, coasting along on the updrafts caused when winds strike the sides of mountain ranges and are deflected upward, or to sail on the thermals, which are currents of warm air. I watch hawk migrations at nearby Montclair, which is in the Watchung Mountain range, or atop the Kittatinny Mountains in northwest New Jersey, or at Hawk Mountain, near Drehersville in Pennsylvania. The hawks that go along the Watchung range apparently come down from New England, coasting along the Watchungs across New Jersey until they reach the Blue Ridge range in eastern Pennsylvania. They take this ridge on down into the Southern states where they pass the winter.

Sometimes on a good day there may be hundreds of broadwinged hawks going by, progressing in so-called "kettles," swirling groups of birds riding a thermal. All species of hawks pass, singly and in groups. Occasionally a bald eagle will wing its majestic way, more occasionally the bright brown-and-white ospreys. Sharp-shinned, red-shouldered, Cooper's, pigeon, and duck hawks add their numbers to the constant stream. I have seen migrating duck hawks deviate ever so slightly from their course to snatch tree swallows out of the air, a difficult feat because of the swallow's agile flight. Added to the hawks are other migrating birds and insects. Hummingbirds, cedar waxwings, evening grosbeaks, monarch butterflies, dragonflies, pursue their routes along the ridges.

CANOE TRIP IN SEPTEMBER. One day in early September I took an eight-mile canoe trip down the Wallkill River with my wife and a friend whom I had known in school. The Wallkill is New Jersey at its best. The stream rises in Lake Mohawk and empties into the Hudson River at Kingston, eighty miles away. In our area it is bordered by willows, maples, and oaks, by swamps and farmlands, by marshy woods and broad fields. It would be a memorable experience to traverse its course even were it not for the many birds that congregate there.

In the whole course of eight miles we saw no other human beings, but we did see many birds. There were almost a thousand blue-winged teal. These graceful ducks wheeled overhead, in flocks of half a hundred or more, or rested on the high waters that had overflowed the normal level of the stream and flooded the adjoining land. As they swung into the sun it seemed as if blue from the sky had fallen on their wings. These teal are the first of our ducks to arrive in the fall, and happily most of them are gone south before the hunting season begins. We saw only one green-winged teal, a later migrant than the blue.

There was a pair of red-headed woodpeckers in one section of the river, a brave sight as the birds flew back and forth across the stream or rested in a tree to make occasional sorties after flies. It was also a great day for killdeer. They were distributed abundantly along the river, with a dozen or more in a single spot or in groups wheeling overhead, uttering their strident cries.

There was no lack of other species. Great blue herons haunted the way, and green and black-crowned night herons were there. Cedar waxwings appeared now and then, taking insects on the wing in the manner of warblers or flycatchers. Black ducks were plentiful, and turkey vultures soared overhead. In one place a pied-billed grebe swam near the shore. It dived under water when we approached, and reappeared an amazingly long distance upstream. The bird propels itself by its feet under water, and seems disinclined to fly, although its wings are strong and swift.

Winter's attractions

Winter bird life holds many attractions. It is almost Christmas before the fall migrants cease drifting away. It is always exciting to find species that are wintering in your area when they should be much farther south. Bird life along the ocean front is interesting, because storms often blow in rarities, such as the dovekies and guillemots.

JERSEY SHORE IN FEBRUARY. Early February is a good time to visit the Jersey shore, but it is best when the wind blows from the northeast, for such a wind brings in the alcids, notably the dovekies, razor-billed auks, murres, guillemots, and hardy sea birds like the eiders. The last time I took such a trip was with the New Jersey Audubon Society. There were some eighty of us, from New

Jersey, New York, and Pennsylvania. We spent Saturday and Sunday at Asbury Park, staying in one of the large hotels there.

We saw 53 species of birds, but there were no rarities among them. The wind blew from the northwest, so none of the alcids were in view. A northeast wind also brings a better chance of finding rare gulls, such as the little, Iceland, glaucous, and black-headed gulls, and the kittiwake. All of these gulls had been seen in the Asbury Park area that winter, and the little and black-headed gulls, both European species, had been seen right opposite the hotel where we were staying.

It is interesting, however, to observe the bird life that is typical at this season of the Jersey shore from the Raritan to the Manasquan Rivers, a stretch that includes not only other little rivers, such as the Shrewsbury, Navesink, and Shark, but also various fresh-water ponds, such as Wreck Pond and Lake Como. The ocean beaches and the jetties provide many species of birds, but so do the moors back from the sand and the wooded areas farther inland.

Eighteen species of ducks were noted over the week end, including the old-squaw, American golden-eye, wood duck, canvasback, and pintail. Two species of grebes and two of loons were found in the company of the ducks and the gulls. A few gannets were seen far out to sea. The small Bonaparte's gulls were common, and there was a sprinkling of great black-backed gulls. The stone jetties that are found irregularly along the ocean front are the haunts of purple sandpipers, and it is possible to approach within a dozen feet of these so-called winter snipe. Robins, singly and in flocks, were numerous. On the way home I stopped at a likely field in Deal and found half a dozen horned larks, always a worth-while addition to any bird list.

CAPE ANN IN DECEMBER. A day in mid-December spent watching birds off the granite promontories of Cape Ann, at Rockport, Massachusetts, and along the barrier beach of Plum Island was very rewarding in the several rarities produced. This region is some three hundred miles from my house by motorcar. Because of its more northern situation, it is visited first by arctic species; because of its exposure to the sea, it is the haven for ocean birds blown in by northeast storms.

Cape Ann juts fifteen miles into the ocean off the northeast shore of Massachusetts. High on its northern edge is Halibut Point, a jagged headland that has been quarried, but not enough to destroy it as a vantage point. You have to dress in sheepskins and woolens, for the wind is sharp and the cold can be severe. At our feet flocks of purple sandpipers flew up and down, stopping to feed upon seaweed exposed on the ledges by the low tide. The three species of scoters shuttled back and forth over the near ocean, and European cormorants, gannets, Holboell's grebes, and red-throated loons joined the traffic in the air. Ducks were numerous too, chiefly blacks, old-squaws, and American golden-eyes.

Andrews Point is near Halibut Point, but at sea level. The water there forms a kind of harbor that is favored by birds in stormy weather. A red-bellied woodpecker had frequented the observation area for some days before our arrival, but was not apparent that day. It is very unusual to see this southern bird so far north. However, almost the first bird that met our view was an American eider. This arctic duck, whose down is one of the best heat-insulating materials known, had seldom ventured into Massachusetts waters in the previous two years. Our bird was a female, rich brown and heavily barred.

While we were watching the eider, a black guillemot flew in front of us and dived out of sight. This is another species from the north, more than a foot long, handsome in black and white. The guillemot is such a hardy diver that it sometimes remains in the arctic throughout the year, feeding under the ice and coming up for a breath wherever it finds an air hole. The guillemots and other alcids (dovekies, Brünnich's murres, and razor-billed auks) prefer Cape Ann because the offshore waters are very deep and hence suitable for these noted divers.

We also saw the Iceland gull at Andrews Point, standing on a nearby ledge with herring and great black-backed gulls. It was a young bird, creamy white all over, and slightly smaller than the herring gull. This is also an arctic species, that in winter may straggle as far south as New Jersey. Two kittiwakes flew across our view, adding another unusual species to our list. The kittiwake is smaller than the other gulls, and while common on the oceans of the world, it seldom ventures near the shore except to nest.

Light fades quickly on winter afternoons, so stopping only to see a Kumlien's gull at nearby Bearskin Neck, we drove on to Newburyport. At this place in the extreme northeastern part of Massachusetts, the Merrimack River broadens into Newburyport Harbor. Plum Island stretches from the harbor ten miles south toward Cape Ann. There were numerous ducks in the harbor and many Bonaparte's gulls. As we proceeded along the harbor toward Plum Island, we traversed familiar fields where a year before I had found upland sandpipers. Now the fields were filled with hunters; I counted fifteen in one area. But by the road was a house, and on top of the chimney perched an immense snowy owl. I learned that this house was occupied by the local game warden, so the owl could have chosen a safer perch. Sometimes the owls alight on haystacks in these fields.

The northern part of Plum Island afforded hundreds of horned grebes and common loons, but it was the southern end, occupied by the Parker River National Wildlife Refuge, that provided the two outstanding rarities. Some distance down the island there is a compound where wild ducks feed, and flying slowly along the edge we sighted a black gyrfalcon. As the bird rested on a stump, we watched it through a 48-power telescope, and could see its markings distinctly. The bird was subsequently seen by a group from the Massachusetts Audubon Society and had been noted previously by Harvard's famed Ludlow Griscom. The gyrfalcon is another arctic bird, bigger than a duck hawk.

Our last rarity was a Pacific loon, which had also been noted some days previously by the Massachusetts bird watchers. It was not far offshore on the ocean side, and similar in appearance to the red-throated loon. The Pacific loon is a Western bird that occurs but rarely on the Atlantic coast. It is sometimes called the arctic loon.

BIRDS AT AIRPORTS. Near where I live are two airports, those of Morristown and Caldwell. Late in November I can go to either and see horned larks and occasional snow buntings and an infrequent Lapland longspur. The birds linger into December, and then leave, to return in late February.

The sight of the snow buntings is very pleasing, for they are quite unafraid, as are so many of the birds from the Far North, and it is possible to approach quite near them. There were three, the last time I saw any, and they kept together, flying rapidly up and down the field and uttering notes that ranged from husky twitterings to musical purrs, and flashing large areas of white on wings, tail, and body. The bunting is whiter than any other songbird, but when the birds alighted on the bare ground the brown and black in their feathers was also noticeable.

There were still two dozen or so horned larks feeding in the grass, but the buntings did not associate with them, appearing rather to enjoy their swift flights up and down the airport. Although the birds breed in regions near the Pole, they take human beings and airplanes for granted. They do not crouch in the grass in the mousy fashion of the horned larks. Rather, they scorn concealment, and if startled, take off in wild, free flight; they seem to enjoy flying, a trait unusual in songbirds.

The number of snow buntings that visits our area each winter is quite unpredictable, but generally they are found along the coastal strip of the state. Charles C. Abbott tells of one winter many years ago when the birds were so common in New Jersey that under the name of "winter reed birds" they were shot and sold in the markets.

I shall always remember another airport, one near Newburyport, for my first upland sandpipers, or upland plovers as they were called then. It was a hot August day, and I was returning from a trip down Plum Island. The grass had been cut at this little airfield along the road, and in the shorn area were these three large inland sandpipers. These and the much smaller buff-breasted sandpipers are the only kinds that you may expect to find in dry fields. I had read accounts of the birds frequenting the moors around Truro and Wellfleet on Cape Cod, and had sought them there unsuccessfully. The birds are a foot long and have notes that are weird, windlike whistles.

CHRISTMAS COUNT. In some ways the Christmas season is the most active time of year for bird clubs, for many of them engage in Christmas censuses. The Christmas count is an old Audubon custom that was instituted more than half a century ago by Frank M. Chapman. Bird watchers are organized into groups that cover specific circular areas fifteen miles in diameter. The census is conducted on a day between Christmas and New Year's.

Last Christmas the Urner Ornithological Club tallied 92 species in my area, including such interesting birds as the Virginia, king, and sora rails in Troy Meadows, the northern and migrant shrikes, and also long-eared, screech, and great horned owls. The Summit Nature Club, nearby, turned up a Nashville warbler, 14 long-eared owls, 4 pileated woodpeckers, and a mockingbird. The Westfield Bird Club included in its count the amazing figure of 17 tree swallows. Tree swallows are usually gone from this area by November, but a flock remained near the reservoir at Oradell throughout the winter of 1940–41, and there are also records of the birds successfully passing the winter on the southern shore of Long Island. This club also included a Baltimore oriole in its census, a bird that is normally much farther south at this season. However, in the winter of 1953–54 at least half a dozen orioles were seen in various parts of my area.

chapter 12 / Bird watching at night

Some of the most fascinating kinds of bird watching are those pursued at night. One of these is to watch the silhouettes of birds as they cross the face of the moon, particularly in the fall. Another is to keep an eye on obstacles to bird migration, such as tall buildings, lighthouses, and airport beacons, and to inspect the victims of collision. It is also instructive to listen to night birds such as owls and whip-poor-wills, and to observe nocturnal creatures such as nighthawks and night herons.

WINGS ACROSS THE MOON. Observation of lunar migrations has become an organized activity only within the last few years, but it is a pastime that any bird watcher can enjoy. All you need is a pair of binoculars or a telescope and a station where you can see the full moon. Your own yard may be as good as any, although you will get better results if your post is on a flyway, such as that which extends over a ridge of hills.

The last time I watched birds passing the moon was on a night in late September when the moon was full. I was in my own back yard, which is well situated, because we live on a ridge 620 feet high that seems to be a natural flyway. There were three other observers with me; I had my 20-power telescope and each of the others had binoculars. We took turns looking through the telescope, because steady scanning is hard on the eyes.

It was a good night, and the birds were streaming past at the rate of 200 an hour. This was faster than the night before, when we counted only 120. If you consider the moon as the face of a clock, the birds on the first night were flying from 9 to 3 o'clock, for the most part, which would seem the direction they would naturally take if headed south. On the following night, at approximately the same time of observation, a great many of the birds were proceeding from 7 to 2 o'clock, as if rising on an updraft or possibly coming from the northeast. Reference is made to earthly, rather than lunar directions, and these would change with the times of observation; those mentioned held true at the hours of my own observations. Sometimes in the fall you see birds flying north, instead of south, but this does not occur very often.

Two hundred birds an hour is a good rate of migration. Some nights you see as few as 60. One observer, living in a different part of the state, told me he had counted only 9 or 10 an hour the same night my friends and I saw 200. It is a help to have your friends join you in this kind of observation if you wish to develop a maximum count, because a person only a short distance away from you may see birds that you miss. This experience may be caused by the angle of observation. It is also desirable to take turns at the telescope. In my experience, a higher power than 20 is not helpful. I have both 40- and 60-power eyepieces for my telescope, but find that they make the image too bright for my eyes and do not permit the full surface of the moon to be included in the field of vision. I have also looked through 5-inch and 8-inch reflecting telescopes with powers up to 65, but do not find them better, either. A filter is required for much moon watching with these big instruments, because the image is so bright it is almost like sun against the naked eye. Here again, only a part of the moon's disk can be observed with such a powerful telescope.

There is much to stir the imagination in the sight of winged silhouettes of herons and ducks and all manner of perching birds that speed across the moon's silver disk. The moon itself is a weird world of craters, mountain ranges, and broad plains. Its silver background for the birds' black silhouettes adds to the mystery of nocturnal migration: What routes do the birds follow? How do they find their way? What obstacles do they encounter in their flight?

Moon watchers were organized by Louisiana State University in 1948 and again in 1952 and 1953 for systematic observation. In the latter years some two hundred stations were established in this country, Canada, and Mexico to amass data on lunar migrations. The lapse between 1948 and 1952 was caused by the enormous difficulty of processing the data collected in the earlier years. It had been found necessary to apply two hours of slide-rule calculations for each hour's observation behind the telescope. Recently, however, solutions have been found for the various computational difficulties. When observations were launched on a large scale in 1952, those participating were bird clubs, museums, classes in ornithology, and astronomical societies, as well as many individuals.

Some of the conclusions made from these studies are that birds do not travel all night long, as previously believed, but that they are on the move mainly during hours near the middle of the night. It was noted that these observations corresponded to a pattern of behavior displayed by European birds confined in electrically wired cages that recorded their hourly activity. It was also found —and this has been obvious to me as it would be to anyone who watched the moon—that, unlike birds in daytime, nocturnal migrants do not group into definite flocks but are scattered throughout the sky. It was also found that a striking correlation existed between air currents and the directions taken by birds.

Some of the questions propounded by the University as being those to which moon watching might provide the answer are these:

Do birds follow rivers at night?

Do birds traveling at night disregard large bodies of water, or do they travel around them?

Do birds avoid cities, where there are few trees?

Do night migrants follow mountain ranges? For example, do the diurnal flights of hawks have any counterpart after sunset?

Do night fliers follow routes that keep them as close as possible to the kind of habitat they like by day, or do they simply head out across the darkness with no concern for the kind of country that lies beneath?

How high do birds fly?

How do birds at night make their way to and from capes and promontories, such as Cape Cod and Cape May?

The moon gazer may be able to contribute to the solution of those questions. But at the very least he will find it is a fascinating and easy kind of bird watching. He may be able to identify certain species against the moon; I have been able to identify herons, ducks, and swallows, and a friend could tell an osprey as it sped by. On some nights you can also hear the birds' cries overhead, and can identify some of them, too, like the distinctive note of the killdeer.

One word of advice: avoid the large telescopes that require a dime in the slot. The first time I tried to watch birds against the moon was in 1934 atop the Empire State Building. I had no glass of my own, but sought to use the huge instrument that is mounted there and that is used ordinarily in the day by sight-seers. However, it was necessary to insert a dime in a slot for a few minutes' use, and I also found the instrument very difficult to focus. The result was that I no sooner found the moon in the telescope than the time ran out and I had to insert another dime. That year being the bottom of the depression, I did not have sufficient dimes to squander in this fruitless pursuit.

HAZARDS ALONG THE WAY. Nocturnal migrants encounter many hazards along the way. If you are near a lighthouse at migration time, for example, it might repay you to search around its base to see if any birds struck it during the night and fell lifeless below. Once when I was near the lighthouse at Cape May Point, the southern extremity of New Jersey, I found on the ground below it myrtle and Cape May warblers, a Wilson's snipe, and several sparrows. The Fire Island Light and the Cape Hatteras Lighthouse have killed hundreds of birds in a single night. A total of 396 individual birds, more than half of them warblers, were killed by striking the former beacon one night. The great light on the top of Mt. Greylock, in the Berkshires, a memorial to Massachusetts war dead, was turned off one year because it confused night migrants, causing them to batter themselves against its heavy glass. Bird ladders, a form of latticework where birds may rest instead of fluttering disastrously against the glass, have been placed below the lights on some English lighthouses, with good results.

In colliding with objects, birds may be killed outright; in some cases only injury to the beak may be sustained. Such injury, while it does not for the time affect the bird's total activity, does prevent its feeding and condemns it to slow death by starvation.

Other tall structures also present hazards to the birds, among them Washington Monument and the Statue of Liberty. Floodlights playing on the shaft of the monument apparently confuse migratory birds, who dash into the powerful beams to their death. One morning 1,400 birds were picked up dead at the base of the Statue of Liberty, having flown into the structure the night before.

In 1953, very early on the morning of September 22, pedestrians on Fifth Avenue and 34th Street in New York City were startled to see dead birds falling all about them. Flocks had crashed into the Empire State Building, and 277 birds of 19 species met their death. These birds were principally warblers; they were on their way to winter homes in the Southern states and Central and South America, and were riding a mass of cold air that passed over New York City. Unfortunately, they followed this air mass when it slipped low under a layer of warm air, thus running afoul of the building. The structure was dark at the time, but it is debatable whether the lives of the feathered migrants would have been spared even if the tower had remained lighted, because of the fatalities known to occur when birds collide with lighthouses and beacons.

The victims in this bird tragedy were of note in that they included a preponderance of unusual species. Six rare Connecticut warblers were included, a score of Tennessee, and numerous bay-breasted warblers. Common species like myrtle and yellow warblers were lacking.

This is only one of several times when the Empire State Building has proved fatal to migrating birds. The last previous large group of fatalities occurred in the early morning of September 11, 1948. Then some 300 individuals, chiefly warblers, were the victims. They included oven-birds, Northern yellow-throats, and redstarts. The accident in this case was attributed to fog that beshrouded the bird's migratory route along the Hudson. That same night unusual numbers of birds were killed against the City Hall in Philadelphia and the airport beacon in Nashville. On October 6, 1954, an amazing total of twenty-eight species among only 127 individual birds flew against the Empire State.

Numerous other hazards beset migrants. Low-flying species, like rails and woodcock, strike fences and houses situated among trees or near woods. High wire fences, such as those that inclose deer parks, are sometimes responsible for the death of wandering grouse.

Unwary geese, ducks, and whistling swans have met their death when they rested at night on the river above Niagara Falls and were swept over the falls. Birds have landed on the hard runways of airports at night, mistaking them in the moonlight for streams of water. They have crashed through the glass tops of greenhouses in similar error. Oil on coastal waters, often a discharge from vessels, sometimes mats the plumage of ducks and other birds, causing them to freeze to death or perish from drowning or starvation. I have seen the carcasses of gannets, the victims of oil, on the sands at Island Beach in my state. Just the other day a reader of mine telephoned from the Jersey shore in perplexity over an immature laughing gull in similar plight, but still alive. The bird was covered with a gummy substance that resisted alcohol, gasoline, chloroform, acetone, and other solvents. When placed in a tub of water it sank like a stone. The bird was taken to a sanctuary and fed there until it finished its molt and got rid of its spoiled plumage.

Forest fires, especially those occurring at night and in the fall, are responsible for the death of many migrants. The birds seem to become fascinated by the light, and have been seen to circle around such fires until overcome by the heat and smoke.

Airplanes are becoming an increasing hazard to night migrants, and ducks, geese, and other birds have collided with planes. In many cases the planes have been damaged, and this has resulted in the development of a windshield that will resist the impact of a heavy bird.

STORMS AT NIGHT. Storms kill untold numbers of birds. Birds will settle in the trees if they sense a storm approaching. One night in September an electrical storm was developing, and before the rain came I could hear the birds alighting in the tall oaks around my house. Flocks may be caught in a storm while crossing large bodies of water, however, or may be blown out to sea by strong winds.

My state is on the Atlantic flyway, and a strong northwest wind may tend to blow the birds out to sea. One night during a recent fall migration, strong offshore winds caused hundreds of small land birds to overshoot Long Island and New Jersey. When day broke, the creatures found themselves over bewildering expanses of water, and sought refuge on fishing boats off the south shore of Long Island and the Jersey coast. Skippers of these craft reported considerable numbers of warblers, kinglets, flickers, and sparrows flitting aimlessly over the ocean. They said the birds were very tame after alighting on a boat, and seemed to be in a state of bewilderment, hopping about and feeding hungrily on flies.

It is this tendency to be blown out to sea by strong northwest winds, and the efforts of the birds to resist it, that makes Cape May in New Jersey such a famed bird sanctuary in the fall. Hurtling down in a southeasterly direction across the state, the birds fight the winds when they reach the ocean, and hug the shore. They make their way gradually southward, eventually congregating at Cape May Point. There they feed and rest before essaying the long hop across Delaware Bay.

One October I was at Cape May during a storm at night and, hearing cries all about me, went out on the beach. Turning my powerful flashlight into the sky, I could see the creatures flying quite low, beating their way back to shore from the sea. I could make out ducks, geese, warblers, and sparrows in this distressed company, besides many shore birds.

So do not hesitate to go out into a storm if you want to see birds, and do not neglect to look about you the morning after a storm.

BIRDS IN A HURRICANE. If the storm is a severe one, of hurricane proportions, you may find rare birds in its aftermath. The hurricane that swept across Long Island and through central New England in September, 1938, carried many oceanic birds with it and affected numerous other species.

For example, a yellow-billed tropic bird was picked up dead in Woodstock, Vermont. This is a white sea bird that is widely distributed in the West Indies, but had never before been recorded in Vermont. A Cory's shearwater, a bird that is unknown in my region away from the ocean and the eastern end of Long Island Sound, was found in Berkshire County, Massachusetts. A Wilson's petrel was found on Lake Ontario, north of Rochester. This little Mother Carey's chicken from the Southern Hemisphere hardly ever goes farther inland than New York Bay.

The red phalarope is a swimming shore bird that rarely comes nearer land than ten or fifteen miles, unless forced in by violent storms. After the storm a specimen was found on the campus of the University of Virginia at Charlottesville. There were other similar records.

There is a theory that birds caught in a cyclonic wind are whirled into its center. There, supported on rising air, they may remain for a long time and be swept very far from their homes. When, exhausted, they drop to earth, the localities they strike should be where the center of the storm has passed. Most of the unusual birds found in New England in September, 1938, were in the path of the center of the hurricane. Shearwaters, petrels, and golden plovers were left in Chatham, Massachusetts, by the "eye" of the hurricane that swept along the Atlantic seaboard on September 11, 1954. Yellow-billed cuckoos in migration were gathered up by this hurricane and thrown back into New England. There, confused and hungry, they thronged the countryside in unprecedented numbers, many perishing from starvation.

The great windstorm of November 25, 1950, blew many dovekies inland. The dovekie is an arctic bird that moves south in winter approximately as far as New Jersey, but generally stays in small flocks in the open sea. One bird was blown inland and was turned over to Mrs. Betty Carnes, then president of the New Jersey Audubon Society. She found the bird hard to feed, but discovered that if she put goldfish in her bathtub the dovekie would dive off the side of the tub after them. It was only faintly interested in sand worms. Mrs. Carnes took the bird to Coney Island and launched it on a wave. The dovekie, being a sea bird, is said to be unable to take off in flight unless it has the crest of a wave to hop from. This is a peculiarity similar to that of the loon, that is said to be unable to rise from land, but must first skid along the surface of water like a hydroplane.

Birds that sing at night

Another form of bird watching at night concerns various nocturnal or seminocturnal birds such as owls, night herons, nighthawks, and whip-poor-wills.

One of the most interesting bird phenomena I know is seen in October at approximately six o'clock when the western sky is yellow and saffron after the setting sun. It occurs at the heronry at Stone Harbor, one of the last dune areas with their original thickets that still exist along the Jersey shore. As you watch the day-feeding birds fly in to roost, they include the American egrets, snowy egrets, and the little blue, great blue, and Louisiana herons. The night-feeding birds—the black-crowned and yellow-crowned night herons—leave at the same time for their nocturnal hunting grounds in the vast salt marshes. One night, with other bird watchers, I kept count. We saw 130 American egrets arrive, along with 211 little blue and 14 Louisiana herons. Leaving the sanctuary at the same time were 133 black-crowned night herons and four of the yellow-crowned species. These great, graceful birds come streaming across the sky, uttering their harsh cries, and land slowly with dangling feet, as do the American egrets, or drop swiftly like the little blue herons.

Occasionally you find other places where the herons roost. One night I saw 93 birds, principally American egrets, fly to roost in an island in the Passaic River near Paterson. It was especially noteworthy to see so many birds congregating on a spot right next to one of the most heavily traveled highways in the state.

You will find it interesting to watch the nighthawks, too. Ordinarily there are not very many of these birds in a particular locality in the summer, but occasionally you hear their sharp "peent" over the city streets, for they like to nest on the roofs of buildings. I shall always remember St. Louis for its nighthawks, for they seemed especially abundant there.

In my region of New Jersey the migration of nighthawks reaches its peak between August 20 and September 10, and sometimes you see remarkable concentrations of them. On one occasion I stood on a high spot in the Watchung Mountains in the evening and looked down toward Newark. The whole valley seemed to be filled with nighthawks; there must have been at least 300. Another observer once saw a flock of 700 along the north Jersey coast in early September.

The whip-poor-will is another bird that is not strictly nocturnal, but you are more likely to hear the bird than see it, and it sings at night. One summer at Cape Cod I pursued a whip-poor-will through the woods, hoping to flash my lantern on it. But the farther I advanced the farther the bird retreated, till eventually I ended in a swamp. If you can't see the whip-poor-will, you can at least listen to it and count its notes. This same whip-poor-will that I chased at Cape Cod used to sing each night hardly a dozen yards from my window. The first summer the bird would utter two hundred or more notes without a stop. The second summer (or maybe it was a different bird) it would persist for only forty.

Startling stories have been told of the bird's remarkable persistence. John Burroughs recorded one instance. He heard a bird strike up near his window, and declares it "laid upon the back of poor Will 1,088 blows," with only a barely perceptible pause here and there. Then it stopped half a minute and began again, uttering 390 calls this time. Burroughs fell asleep in the middle of the next count.

One of my correspondents wrote that his family had lived on its homestead in nearby Boonton since 1674, and that for several generations its name had been known as Wawonaissa Farm, which, he said, is an Indian name for whip-poor-will. He wrote that over the past sixty-five years he and members of his family had counted, in the hundreds, the repetitions of that call by the bird. He wrote: "The best record we have was a count made in the early morning of June 26, 1945, by my daughter, who counted 1,409 repetitions of the call by a single bird close to the house. The calls ran at about two per second, and she lost count at that number because she was unable to keep up the count in such rapid succession. The bird continued for some time afterward."

OWLS. Success in finding owls consists of knowing their calls and being acquainted with the places they frequent. This information can best be obtained from other bird watchers. My first experience with a long-eared owl was on the military reservation at Picatinny Arsenal. One night I heard a noise that sounded like the mewing of a kitten in the vicinity of an area of pine trees. I walked in that direction, believing an animal might have become lost. Soon I found that the mewing changed direction with such speed that the sound must have come from a bird. The long-eared owl is sometimes known as the cat owl because of its distinctive cry.

You can see the short-eared owls at dusk in the tidal marshes along the Jersey shore, and not far from me is an extensive swamp where a few barred owls make their haunts. The best way to rouse one is to enter the swamp along an elevated boardwalk there, and after you have penetrated to the area where the bird is heard, imitate the call. This consists of making a noise like a barking dog. More often than not, you will hear the owl's answering hoots coming from the swamp. The bird's preference for swamps has given it the local name of swamp owl.

Owls and other birds are also heard before daybreak. Friends of mine on days of strenuous birding have identified as many as 50 birds by their notes alone, in the dark of early morning. One of the most inspiring experiences in bird watching is to arise before the birds on a May day and listen as the various species add their notes to the chorus that soon swells into the unparalleled music of a spring morning.

chapter 13 / Bird banding

When you become so expert that you can identify without question all the birds in your locality, you are then ready for an advanced activity known as *bird banding*. You don't necessarily have to be a bird bander, and many noted ornithologists never engage in this program. However, it has been called the most important activity of American bird watchers. It holds fascinating interest for the bird enthusiast, can produce important scientific results, and can conveniently be done entirely within the confines of one's own back yard.

It has been said that you must be thoroughly competent to identify all the species of birds in your locality. You cannot band birds without a permit from the federal government, and you cannot get the permit unless you are vouched for by three well-known ornithologists. The value of bird banding consists in tracing the movements of birds through numbered bands affixed to their legs. Obviously, this operation would have no value if birds were not identified correctly.

Bird banding opens the door to an intimate knowledge of wild birds. One of its strongest appeals is the opportunity it provides to hold in hand and become closely acquainted with feathered creatures. Moreover, experience has shown that the trapping, handling, and banding of wild birds does not harm them.

History of banding

Attempts to mark wild birds so that they could be identified began very early in the last century. Numbered aluminum or colored plastic bands are now most commonly used, but other devices have included little bells, bits of colored yarn, paint on some of the feathers, plain rings, and wire. The earliest record of a banded bird was that of a great gray heron (Ardea cinerea) captured in Germany in 1710. The bird wore on one leg a metal ring that had been placed there several years before in Turkey. However, nothing of much importance was accomplished in bird banding until 1899. In that year a Danish schoolmaster, C. C. Mortensen, began systematically to band storks, teals, starlings, and a few birds of prey. His success attracted the attention of European ornithologists, and bird banding, or "ringing" as it is called in the Old World, began in most of the European countries.

The first birds banded in the United States appear to have been pewees. Audubon, while he was living on Perkiomen Creek, near Philadelphia, fastened silver wires to the legs of a brood of pewees while they were still in the nest, and some of the birds returned the following year to breed in the locality where they were born. Dr. Paul Bartsch of the Smithsonian Institution was the first bander in North America to use numbered metal bands. In 1902 and 1903 he banded some hundred black-crowned night herons in the District of Columbia. Largely through the efforts of Dr. L. J. Cole, who first brought to the attention of American ornithologists the possibilities in banding, the American Bird Banding Association was formed in 1909. By 1920 greater resources were needed for the expanding program, so bird banding was taken over as an official project by the U.S. Biological Survey (now the Fish and Wildlife Service). An agreement was soon made between the United States and Canada to use a common set of numbers for banding operations. In the United States the Migratory Bird Treaty Act authorizes banding as an activity to obtain information useful in the protection of migratory birds and in the regulation of the migratory game bird hunting seasons.

Objectives

The purposes of bird banding are to collect scientific data with which to work out the migrations, dispersals, and ages of birds and study the behavior of individuals.

MIGRATION. In respect to migration, banding records help to show the routes followed by birds from their breeding to their wintering grounds and return. They also show where these grounds are, as the first intimation we had of the wintering area of the chimney swift came in 1944 from thirteen leg bands recovered in Peru from birds banded in the United States and Canada. Times of arrival and departure, effect of weather on travel, information as to whether the males, females, and young travel together or separately, and data as to whether there is much return to the same nesting locality are other areas where banding records shed light.

DISPERSAL. Banding gives facts on the dispersal of birds that do not return to the area where they were hatched. The strength of the homing instinct and the proportion of males and females returning to the same nesting sites are other subjects for inquiry under this head.

AGE OF BIRDS. Banding supplies facts on the normal longevity of different species. The vast majority of local birds banded are never retaken, suggesting that many fall victims to the countless dangers that beset them.

PERSONALITY. Banding affords an opportunity to study birds as individuals in respect to habits, appearance, and manners.

OTHER OBJECTIVES. Banding records throw light on reasons for the preference of birds for different types of environment, the length of time that the unity of the bird family is maintained, the permanence of bird matings, and many problems concerning plumage.

Results

Only a few items will be listed here from the many thousands that have resulted from bird-banding activities.

Knowledge has been developed that marks the arctic tern as the bird that enjoys the greatest amount of sunlight each year of all living animals, because it makes the longest migration. It makes a round trip of 25,000 miles each year, nesting near the Arctic Circle and wintering in the Antarctic. This information is based upon the following recovery of bands:

A bird banded in July, 1913, in Maine was found dead in August, 1917, in Nigeria, West Africa.

A bird banded in Labrador in June, 1927, was found dead in October, 1927, in western France.

A bird banded in July, 1928, in Labrador was found dead in November, 1929, in Natal, South Africa.

A bird banded in July, 1935, on Machias Seal Island, New Brunswick, was captured in October, 1935, in western France.

A bird banded in July, 1947, on Machias Seal Island, New Brunswick, was found dead in November, 1948, at Cape Province, South Africa.

A bird banded in July, 1948, on Machias Seal Island, New Brunswick, was found dead in September, 1948, near Sutherland, Scotland.

Banding has produced evidence of the unusual flights accomplished by other species. On September 7, 1951, a pintail was banded in Labrador. Eighteen days later it was shot in southern England. Another pintail was banded in North Dakota on August 27, 1939, and recovered January 10, 1940, in Colombia, South America. Another bird of the same species was banded at Tule Lake, California, on August 16, 1949, and recovered on November 15 of the same year in the Cook Islands, New Zealand. And still another, banded at Maui Island, Hawaii, on October 21, 1951, was shot on September 10, 1952, near Edmonton, Alberta, Canada.

Information is also obtained about the lives of individual species. For example, S. Prentiss Baldwin, a Cleveland lawyer (who did pioneer work in bird banding between 1914 and 1919) exposed the marital irregularities of the house wren. His banding records showed that these birds commonly change their mates at different seasons and that the female who raised a brood with one male early in the spring shunted him off for another mate for her second brood. The male is also unfaithful, deserting his first wife for other mates in one nesting period. These studies have also shown that the male wrens arrive before the females, singing vociferously as they inspect nesting sites, often removing the contents of last year's boxes. These observations were based upon repeated capture of banded birds on their nests.

One of the most fascinating questions answered by bird banding is how long birds live in the wild. Such information comes from records such as the following: A purple martin was found dead underneath the birdhouse in which it had been banded fourteen years previously. A red-winged blackbird banded in New York was shot fourteen years later in North Carolina. A hunter in Newfoundland shot a black duck that had been tagged seventeen years before at Cape Cod, Massachusetts. A pintail duck banded in Utah was killed twelve years later in California. An arctic tern was banded on Cape Cod in 1929 and found dead in 1951. A record for longevity in the wild was set by a Caspian tern that was banded as a nestling on Little Hat Island, near St. James, Michigan, in 1925, and shot in Ohio in 1951, a full twenty-six years after banding.

Data derived from banding operations indicate heavy mortality among young birds and a greatly lessened rate once they have achieved maturity. Richard H. Pough, in his *Audubon Water Bird Guide*, has indicated in the text for each bird he describes the maximum longevity achieved in cases where records are available. He points out that these figures represent the maximum potential life spans in only a few cases. Some of the ages he reports are as follows: *

* From *Audubon Water Bird Guide*, by RICHARD H. POUGH, copyright 1951 by Doubleday and Company, Inc.

Common shearwater	12	Golden eagle	30
Brown pelican	12½	Gallinule	5½
Gannet	16½	Red-backed sandpiper	5
Great blue heron	15	Herring gull	17
Canada goose	9	(49 in captivity)	
Mallard	15	Common tern	18
Red-tailed hawk	13½	Mourning dove	9

Smaller birds have shorter lives. A white-breasted nuthatch may live for only four years; a downy woodpecker, and wood thrush, for five.

Scope

Approximately seven million birds have been banded in North America since the program began. An additional three to four hundred thousand are banded each year. The number of persons engaged in banding varies from year to year, but has been about two thousand of late. Most of these banders are in the United States, but others are in Canada, Hawaii, and the West Indies.

From the total banding some five hundred thousand returns and recoveries have been obtained, or approximately 7 per cent. More than six hundred species have been banded, with the following subjects the most popular:

Mallard	471,047	Herring gull	219,420
Chimney swift	456,882	Song sparrow	189,794
Common tern	396,754	Robin	158,797
Pintail	242,237	Starling	154,269
	Purple grackle	154,217	

The number of birds captured in a day may range from a few individuals to more than two hundred. Such individuals may include many species. Frank P. Frazier, of Montclair, New Jersey, president of the Eastern Bird Banding Association, banded 71 species in 1953. He tagged 38 species in May, 1952, and 34 in May and in September, 1953. At one banding station in Georgia 37 species were taken one year between January and April. One chipping sparrow was caught in the same trap at this station 54 times during one season. A fox sparrow was caught 165 times during one winter. In Minnesota a song sparrow was taken from the trap 55 times between April 14 and 30; in May it was caught 106 times.

At one time bird banders were composed almost entirely of amateurs, but of late years the number of professional wildlife workers has increased substantially. The amateurs still purchase their own equipment and donate their own time, but the cash value of their contributions is now more than matched by the government agencies operating bird-banding programs. Many states now have federal aid projects that involve banding waterfowl, doves, and other birds.

Kinds of banding

There are three general types of bird banding: the banding of fledglings, the operation of traps, and color banding.

BANDING FLEDGLINGS. The banding of fledglings is most successful when conducted in the great sea-bird colonies, where the birds can be banded in large numbers. Birds that nest in colonies and offer good opportunities for wholesale banding are gulls, terns, pelicans, and cormorants. Such banding has provided information on birds that cross the Atlantic, such as terns and kittiwakes. It has also yielded records on the longevity of birds. For example, in 1939 a black-headed gull was caught in Central Europe twenty-five years after it had been banded as a nestling.

Banding of nestlings has been successful to a degree with gulls and terns, because the bodies of these birds are often washed ashore and their rings recovered. Birds that are often shot, such as hawks, owls, and herons, also yield their rings. Generally, the banding of nestlings is discouraged, because it may lead to injury to the birds from predators or other causes.

Among ordinary birds, from 1 to 4 are subsequently retaken out of every 100 trapped, while among ducks, which are shot and their bands turned in, the recovery runs from 12 to 20. Jack Miner at Kingsville, Ontario, banded ducks and geese attracted to his refuge. He stated that 40 per cent of the birds he tagged in the fall returned the following spring. Geese bearing his band were taken in 23 states.

TRAPPING STATIONS. Most bird banders operate traps in their own yards, banding adult birds. The traps are situated conveniently near one's house, and can be watched by several members of the family.

The number of birds banded that are recaptured in some subsequent season varies for the species, but one bander in South Carolina found that approximately 16 per cent of 12,000 birds returned. The returns were highest, 19.6 per cent, for chipping sparrows. Such findings have shown that certain birds winter or breed in the same locality year after year.

Bird banders have found that if they move their traps about they enormously increase their chances for returns. Some bird banders study a single species in an area by trying to trap all the individuals of a given species in that area.

One of the greatest trapping stations I have seen is the one maintained by Dr. O. L. Austin at South Wellfleet on Cape Cod. I frequently pass the summer in that community, and visit his Ornithological Laboratory. He has on his many acres wire traps that are some 8 feet high and 8 feet square on the base. In late summer the cages are filled with young cowbirds and red-winged blackbirds. Dr. Austin has banded vast numbers of common and roseate terns, his total in the former standing at 386,752 at the beginning of 1951.

COLOR MARKING. In color marking the emphasis is changed from trapping to watching. In this operation, colored celluloid bands are used. They can be affixed to a bird's leg in various combinations. The number of combinations possible is 1,536 if you use only four differently colored bands (yellow, red, green, and black, for instance) in conjunction with the numbered metal ring. This would enable you to identify by sight 1,536 different birds, thus eliminating the catching and recatching that would otherwise be necessary for a positive identification of an individual bird and that would cause inconvenience for the bird student and some distress for the bird. Colored bands have contributed to studies of bird behavior in the cases of chickadees, white-breasted nuthatches, black-crowned night herons, mockingbirds, and song sparrows. Other ways of marking birds are to glue colored feathers to their tails or to paint certain feathers. The latter method, however, loses its effectiveness when the birds molt.

Color-band identification helps to determine a bird's predilection for certain territory, the part played by the sexes in incubating eggs or feeding the young, the relation of song to nesting, and other matters.

How to become a bander

There are five considerations for those who wish to engage in bird banding:

1. They can submit an application on a blank (Form 3–481) obtained from the Bird-Banding Office, Patuxent Research Refuge, Laurel, Maryland, and in Canada from the Chief, Dominion Wildlife Service, Ottawa, Ontario.
2. The program is a voluntary one, in which the bander donates his time and pays for his equipment, and receives neither compensation nor reimbursement from the government. The Service, however, provides at no cost to the bander the bands and report forms.
3. An applicant must be at least eighteen years old.
4. He must be thoroughly competent to identify positively all the local species of birds.
5. This ability must be vouched for by three recognized ornithologists or banders.

Banding operations

BANDS. The Fish and Wildlife Service provides without charge aluminum bands that come in fourteen sizes to fit some 800 different species of birds. Inside diameters range from .083 inch for bands suitable for warblers to .875 inch for eagles, swans, and other big birds. The Service furnishes bird banders with a list of all birds that shows the appropriate size of band to use on each species. Bands of all sizes are issued in full strings of 100 each. They are of a split-ring type that are opened sufficiently to be placed around the leg and closed again with pliers so that the ends meet evenly and tightly. All the official aluminum bands bear a serial number and an address, such as "Write F & W Serv, Wash D.C., USA."

TYPES OF PERMITS. There are four types of federal permits, the type being stated on the face of each permit card: migratory nongame; migratory nongame and doves; migratory nongame, doves, shore birds, rails, and allies; migratory (game) birds, which permits the banding of all species of birds, including ducks and geese, but which also restricts banding usually to specific areas such as refuges, parks, and sanctuaries.

Permits. Current permits for banding in the United States are 8½ x 11 inch forms (Form 3–475a) issued by the Fish and Wildlife Service of the U.S. Department of the Interior.

State permits. Most states require banders to hold a state permit in addition to the federal permit. The latter is not valid without the former.

BANDING SCHEDULES. Reports concerning birds that have been banded are made to the Bird-Banding Office in Laurel, Maryland. These reports are called schedules. The banding year runs from May 1 through the following April 30, and most of the schedules should be submitted to Laurel by June 30 of each year.

Preparation of schedules. There are rather rigid specifications for the preparation of schedules. The bands should be listed in numerical order, the bander's permit number should be shown, the official species number of the American Ornithologists' Union should be given, common and scientific names of the birds should be provided. The age of the birds should be designated.

RETURN CARDS. Another form (Form 3–137) is used to report birds that return to the station where they have been banded, as well as the recovery of the operator's own birds in the immediate vicinity of his banding station.

REPORTED RECOVERIES. All recoveries of birds at localities other than the banding station by persons other than the bander are reported by letter to the Bird-Banding Office at Laurel. The letter should state the full number of the band; if possible, the band should be secured and returned too. The species of the bird, where found, and how obtained (shot, trapped, found dead, injured) should also be reported. The Bird-Banding Office reports to the original bander of the bird that his bird has been recovered, and sends a carbon copy to the person who sent in the recovery report.

TRAPS AND NETS. Various types of cage traps that take the birds alive without injuring them are used for banding. The first trap used was the government sparrow trap, devised by the Biological Survey to capture house sparrows. The bander has to make or buy his own traps. Sometimes nets are used. It is the policy to tend traps and band and release the birds the first thing in the morning, at intervals of not more than three hours during the day, and just at dusk so birds do not remain in the traps over-night.

The matter of bait is also important; food requirements of birds vary greatly, and in order to take them one must cater to their tastes.

Anyone can assist

Persons finding bird bands can aid the program by reporting by mail every such band. They can examine injured and dead birds found along highways or those washed up on shores. Hunters should examine their kill to see whether or not the birds are banded. Banded birds are sometimes caught accidentally in muskrat traps or in fishermen's nets.

GOVERNMENT COOPERATION. The Fish and Wildlife Service at Patuxent Research Refuge, Laurel, Maryland, issues permits, bands, report forms, and instruction manuals to banders, and provides post cards for requisitioning supplies.

READING MATERIAL. If you are interested you should first write to Patuxent and ask for Leaflet WL-235, *Bird Banding*, by SETH Low, revised as of November, 1951. The Bird-Banding Office at Patuxent will send you copies of BIRD BANDING NOTES, issued for the benefit of bird-banding cooperators. One of these in partic-ular, Vol. 4, No. 2, August, 1949, has basic data on how to be-come a bander and carry on a program. Then you should sub-scribe to BIRD-BANDING, a publication that was founded in 1930 and is the journal of those engaged in the activity.

BIRD-BANDING ASSOCIATIONS. Anyone interested in bird banding may like to join one of the associations devoted to that activity. There are four: Eastern Bird-Banding Association, whose
president is Frank Frazier, 424 Highland Avenue, Upper Montclair, New Jersey; the Inland Bird-Banding Association, led by
Karl E. Bartel, 2528 W. Collins Street, Blue Island, Illinois;
the Northeastern Bird-Banding Association, whose president is
Charles H. Blake, of Lincoln, Massachusetts; and the Western
Bird-Banding Association, whose business manager is Francis H.
Boynton, 163 W. State Street, Pasadena 2, California. The North-
eastern Bird-Banding Association publishes *Bird-Banding*, a quar-
terly, and the Eastern Association publishes the bimonthly *EBBA
News*. The Inland Association publishes *Inland Bird-Banding
News*, a bimonthly.

Reading reference

Bird-Ringing, by R. M. LOCKLEY and ROSEMARY RUSSELL,
Crosby Lockwood & Son, Ltd., London, 1953, 119 pp., illus. This
excellent book tells the history of bird-ringing, value of the operation, techniques of ringing and trapping, and describes rings,
records, and field equipment.

chapter 14 / Collecting old nests

The first bird's nest I ever collected was a black-throated green warbler's nest that was still in a spruce we bought one Christmas. I later inquired of the dealer and found that his trees had come from Nova Scotia.

Everyone has probably collected a few nests, but this is an interesting phase of bird watching that merits some attention. I refer particularly to the collection of nests that the birds are done with; I do not favor taking nests that have been completed but not used, on the supposition that the frustrated birds will immediately build new structures. This practice is a needless interference with the creatures' domestic routine, and serves no useful purpose that could not be served by waiting for the nest to be used and abandoned.

Why collect nests?

The essential purpose in collecting old nests is to study their structure and materials. The fruits of such study add to the scientific substance of one large phase of ornithology. Such study reveals to the bird watcher not only what others know, such as what kinds of plant, animal, and mineral materials go into the building of nests, and where and how they are constructed, but it may also reveal facts not previously known. Such facts relate to the birds' adjustment to changing conditions. What, for instance, replaces horses' hairs in nests built in areas where horses have disappeared? To what extent is metal being used in birds' nests; bits of rusty poultry fence, paper clips, and other items? Birds exhibit remarkable ability to adapt their habits to changing conditions, but to what extent is this the adaptability of the individual and to what extent a new habit of the species?

UNUSUAL SITES. Birds that occupy nesting boxes number half a hundred species, and it is noteworthy that many of them are birds that normally nest in cavities in trees, such as bluebirds, woodpeckers, owls, nuthatches, and so on. As dead trees disappear from the landscape, these species must be satisfied with artificial nesting sites.

However, the remarkable ability of birds to build wherever a suitable situation presents itself and irrespective of the habits of its species is demonstrated almost daily in the nesting season. In Connecticut a man lost his model airplane in the woods, and when he discovered it he found birds had nested in the cockpit. In Bexhill, England, a blackbird that laid its eggs in a nest on a farm tractor refused to budge even when the tractor bumped around the fields. A family of robins was raised on a coil of insulated wire at the Army depot in Schenectady, and the house wrens that have built their nests in the pockets of scarecrows or in old coats and trousers hanging outside are probably legion. In Bernardsville, New Jersey, a robin built its nest under the front fender of a pick-up truck, and in Independence, California, a hummingbird attached its nest to the electric-light cord above an open bulb. A house sparrow established some kind of record in this respect by nesting for ten years in a flowerpot on the fire escape of an apartment in the Bronx.

UNUSUAL MATERIALS. Birds display ingenuity also in the materials they use. The well-known proclivity of the crested flycatcher for putting a snake skin in its nest is almost matched by other birds' choices. It is well known that many forest fires are set by birds that carry lighted cigarettes to their nests. House wrens are very catholic in their tastes. One in Muskegon, Michigan, was found popping into a nesting box with a bright object in its beak. Came fall and the secret was out: 156 pieces of metal, in addition to conventional nesting materials, had gone into the box. They included 6 safety pins, 4 paper clips, 28 bobby pins, 11 hairpins, 1 garter slide, 27 small nails, 1 fishhook, 1 screw eye, 38 staples, and 39 miscellaneous pieces of wire. I once found a wren's nesting box in my own back yard filled with pieces of wire that the birds had picked up along the chicken run. Ravens near Dalhart, Texas, hunting about for nesting materials, could find no sticks or straws, but they did come upon a pile of barbed wire, rusted into small pieces. The birds built five all-metal homes out of this prickly material.

Birds that nest in cities are hard put to it to find adequate nesting stuff, and both house sparrows and rock doves employ paper clips, cellophane wrappings from cigars, and any scraps of paper they can find, even occasional dollar bills. The Eastern chipping sparrow builds a delicate, cleverly interwoven nest of fine grass and rootlets, lined with hair of horse, cow, or deer. What happens when there are no horses, deer, or cows around, as there are not in most suburban communities where chipping sparrows abound? A correspondent of the *Rural New Yorker* tells of one expedient. The woman's son had a woolen blanket from which he was inseparable when sleepy or tired. The child found great comfort in pulling off bits of wool, which he rolled into balls of fuzz, calling them his "mice." The other children came into the house one day, exclaiming over a chipping sparrow's nest they had found. The bird had used the youngest child's "mice" as a soft, warm lining. Another chipping sparrow's nest found by this same woman was lined with hair—not of the horse, but of the woman herself—brushings that had been swept or dusted out of the door.

USUAL MATERIALS. A study of nests is interesting not only because of the unusual materials birds may employ, but also because of the stuff that it is their wont to use. The indigo bunting uses fine grasses, leaves, and a few weeds with a lining of feathers or hairs. The cup-shaped nest of the yellow-throated vireo is beautifully adorned with lichens and cocoons, held in place with caterpillars' silk and spiders' webs. The ring-necked duck lines its nest with dark gray down, frequently mixed with its own breast feathers. The chimney swift constructs a semicircular basket of twigs, which it glues together and attaches to a chimney or similar structure with its own glutinous saliva. The black-throated blue warbler makes its nest of bark strips, rootlets, grasses, vines, twigs, and spiders' webs, all neatly lined with fine black rootlets, and decorated on the outside with corky bits of wood and woolly parts of cocoons. Pieces of dead wood are placed in the bottom of the nest.

CONSTRUCTION METHODS. The art and skill of the birds in constructing their homes also holds considerable fascination for the bird watcher. The robin and wood thrush are masons of a kind, laying a foundation of mud for their structure of grass, twigs, rootlets, and various other materials. The yellow warbler's nest is often placed in forks of bushes or saplings, and is a cup-shaped structure, compactly made of silver-gray plant fibers, fine grasses, and many other substances. Sometimes an especially deep nest will be found; it has resulted from the bird's building a second floor to cover and leave unhatched a cowbird's egg. This parasite has a particular fondness for leaving its eggs in the yellow warbler's nest.

The hummingbird's nest has been praised for its delicate structure, being covered so perfectly with lichens as to appear a mere protuberance on the branch on which it is placed. The blue-gray gnatcatcher has a like faculty for making its nest appear like a knot on a limb.

How to find birds' nests

There are three good ways to find birds' nests: (1) look for them in the fall after the leaves have gone; (2) discover them while the birds are still nesting; (3) pay neighborhood children to collect them for you.

NEST HUNTING IN THE FALL. Thoreau wrote in his diary: "Another bright Winter's day, to the woods to see what birds' nests are made of." Those who follow the example of the sage of Walden Pond may go out as early as the leaves have fallen, revealing to plain view the robin's structure of mud and grass, the pensile basket of the oriole, the interwoven nest of the vireo. The casual observer can count a dozen of last summer's nests along any tree-lined street.

I usually carry a heavy, sharp knife when on bird walks in the fall and winter, for there are ample opportunities to gather nests from bushes and saplings by cutting away the supporting wood. It is always surprising to me when abroad at this season to find so many birds' nests where I never suspected them. They are high in trees of your own yard, across the street in a neighbor's hedge, in the rose arbor where you never noticed bird activity in the summer.

WATCH NESTING BIRDS. Another way to find nests is to watch nesting birds, and after the nest has been located, mark the spot and collect the nest later in the season when it has been abandoned. Many small birds have to make so many visits to their nests in order to satisfy the voracious appetites of their young that they give away the nest's location. However, birds of prey are more difficult to trace, for it is their habit to leave their chicks for longer intervals. The singing stations of male birds may give an approximate notion of the location of their nests. This process may take much patient looking with binoculars, or once a likely area has been staked out, may take painstaking search of underbrush for the nests of birds that build in the lower levels of the woods. Some birds, such as killdeer, disclose the sites of their nests by feigning injury when you are near them.

Nests that are collected after being first sighted when in use hold more interest than others because you know something of the history of the nest and the bird. You may take notes that you may later attach to the nest, concerning the time required for its construction, whether made by one or both sexes, whether both sexes assisted in incubation, the number of days the young were in the nest, and so forth.

BUYING NESTS. If you are trying to make a collection of nests of all the birds that breed in a particular area, or merely a large collection of nests, you may have to rely somewhat upon the help of children. Boys and girls are inveterate wanderers through woods and have a good faculty for combing the underbrush. If you offer a reward for particular kinds of nests that are missing from your collection, you may be able to procure these new ones. It is desirable to make such an offer only after the birds have done nesting, as otherwise some avaricious youngsters may take nests even with eggs in them.

How to identify nests

Most of the field guides to birds have good descriptions of birds' nests. There is a book solely on the subject: *Birds' Nests*, by RICHARD HEADSTROM.

If you see the bird on the nest, there is not much difficulty in identifying it, but nests have certain characteristics that enable you to identify them even after the bird has flown. The size of the nest is an obvious clue to the size of the bird. The environment in which the nest is found is another clue, whether dry woods, edge of a marsh, open field, or whatever. The location of the nest should be considered, whether on the ground, in a bush, or high in a tree. Type of construction is also important in identification, whether the nest is open or closed, shaped like a cup or a platform. Depth of nest is important, and finally, the kinds of nesting materials used.

How to keep nests

There are several ways to keep nests or records of nests. One is to keep the nest itself, provided your wife will let you clutter up the house with them. Some nests, such as the stockings of the oriole, the pendent baskets of the vireos, and the thick-walled cup of the yellow warbler, may be taken with the branch or crotch of the sapling to which they are attached. Still other nests, such as the robin's, may be lifted readily off the large branch or fork of a tree in which they are placed.

WIRE BASKETS. Other nests present more difficulty. Frank Chapman suggests placing such a nest in a kind of wire basket so that it can be held together. It is made by twisting two pieces of heavy wire, painted brown, into a letter X. The wires should be bent upward about midway between the point of intersection and the end of the arm. Then fine wire should be wound around the four horizontal arms of the frame until its bottom looks like a spider's web. The nest is placed in this rough frame, and the winding of fine wire continued until the nest is firmly bound.

A man I know who has a large collection of nests places them in sizable shallow boxes, in which he has made suitably sized compartments, somewhat after the fashion of compartments in an egg carton.

PHOTOGRAPHIC AND OTHER RECORDS. The bird watcher may find it more convenient to keep a record of his nest rather than the nest itself. He may do this by making photographs, a method that has the great advantage of showing the environment in which the nest is built. This is a significant matter, and one which is not conveyed merely by the nest. These photographs may be mere record shots taken with a miniature camera, or may be careful and artistic representations.

The bird watcher may be content merely to take written notes. These notes should give details as to materials used, site and environment, and nature of construction, especially if anything unusual was noted, and should include any details that may have been gathered about the nesting activity if that was observed. In such record keeping it might be desirable for the student to compare his nests with the descriptions given of those for species in standard manuals, in order to emphasize in his observations any deviations from the normal. This practice will relieve him of recording anew facts that have already been recorded by others.

One nest collection

One of the correspondents to my column in the *Newark Sunday News* is Edward M. Wisner of Elberon, New Jersey. He has collected 126 nests of different species that breed in the state. He teaches school, and uses his collection in biology classes. The first 50 nests in his collection are listed here as being representative of those that might constitute the beginning of any persistent bird watcher's collection:

Blackbird, Red-winged	Rail, Clapper
Bluebird	Rail, Virginia
Bob-white	Redstart
Bunting, Indigo	Robin
Cardinal	Sparrow, Chipping
Catbird	Sparrow, Field
Chat, Yellow-breasted	Sparrow, Song
Chickadee, Black-capped	Sparrow, Swamp
Crow	Starling
Cuckoo, Yellow-billed	Swallow, Barn
Dove, Mourning	Swallow, Rough-winged
Flycatcher, Alder	Tanager, Scarlet
Flycatcher, Crested	Thrasher, Brown
Goldfinch	Thrush, Wood
Grackle, Purple	Towhee
Hummingbird	Vireo, Red-eyed
Jay, Blue	Vireo, White-eyed
Killdeer	Warbler, Chestnut-sided
Kingbird	Warbler, Hooded
Lark, Horned	Warbler, Magnolia
Meadowlark	Warbler, Yellow
Oriole, Baltimore	Woodcock
Oriole, Orchard	Wren, House
Oven-bird	Wren, Long-billed Marsh
Phoebe	Yellow-throat

chapter 15 / Photographing birds

People who take pictures of birds are either primarily bird watchers with a secondary interest in photography, or primarily photographers with a secondary interest in birds. Accordingly, some will be interested in photographing birds mainly because of the significant records of bird behavior they obtain. They will not take pictures unless these pictures record incidents in life histories, or unless they illustrate the bird in its habitat, or serve some other useful scientific purpose. The photographers who are primarily artists are not deeply concerned with the subject from the point of view of its scientific value; they seek pictures that are beautiful in pose and composition, or that arrest some striking activity.

Just as there is no single approach to the purposes of bird photography, so there is no one prescription for photographic equipment. Different purposes demand different cameras. An attempt will be made here to describe briefly some of the uses of bird photography and some of the devices and pieces of equipment that may be employed.

What to take

Bird watchers who want photographs that are merely charming pictures, or that recall for them experiences with birds that they wish to remember, have the widest range of subjects. The robin on the nest, the gull on the sands, the jay in the apple blossoms, all these and infinitely more produce appealing bird subjects.

Bird watchers who wish more ornithological purpose to their photography choose more specific targets.

NESTING BIRDS. One of the most popular subjects is nesting birds. It is interesting for the persistent photographer to take a whole series of photographs of the nesting cycle of the robin, for instance, showing the building of the nest, the hatching of the eggs, the feeding of the young, and their eventual departure from the nest.

FEEDING-STATION VISITORS. Feeding habits of birds also make good subjects. The photographer could take many of these shots from his own window, showing how birds behave around feeding stations, how they attack suet, how they drink and bathe. A useful series might be taken on the bathing habits of various birds, perhaps starting with that notable bather, the robin.

COURTSHIP BEHAVIOR. There are many other classes of subjects. One is the courting behavior of birds. It is possible for the beginner to capture in his camera some of the courtship antics of the flicker, for example. Or he may photograph birds singing in announcement of their rights to certain territory, or engaged in specialized activities such as "anting," wherein they rub ants over their plumage, presumably to rid their bodies of lice.

It is well for the beginner to start by taking pictures of birds that are easy to approach, as chickadees.

Where to take pictures

One of the best places to photograph birds is at feeding stations. Birds attend the stations periodically, so the camera can be set up to catch them when they arrive. Or one can build a blind in which to conceal himself near the station, or hide behind a curtain and snap his subjects when they alight by a window. I fix a camera on a tripod and place it close to a tree on whose trunk I have fastened suet. By running a stout thread from the camera to my study window, I can photograph downy and hairy woodpeckers, nuthatches, starlings, and other species that peck at the suet. Both submerged and elevated bird baths and pools are similar focal points of interest for birds.

BIRDS AT FAVORITE PERCHES. It is possible to attract birds at the shore or at park lakes by offering them food. I have seen birds that are normally shy, such as the coot, come out of the water to take bread with the same alacrity displayed by park mallards. Birds also have favorite roosts or perches, and if you focus your camera on such spots you may get unusual pictures. This is especially true of certain water or shore birds, such as gulls, cormorants, and sandpipers.

The nest is another place that is photographed successfully, because the birds return to it periodically. Especially good nest pictures may be secured after the young have been hatched for a few days and the parental instincts of the adults are so strong and their feeding activities so arduous that they are less likely to be disturbed by intruding photographers. They will tolerate a camera at this time and be less suspicious of a blind. Never cut branches away from a nest in order to photograph it. Tie back the branches and release them after you have taken your pictures. Otherwise the nestlings are needlessly exposed to predators and hot sunlight.

Use of a blind

A *blind*, or a *hide* as the British call it, is a device that conceals the photographer, allowing him to be near a bird without arousing the latter's suspicions.

LOW-LEVEL BLIND. A simple blind consists of canvas or burlap thrown over four upright posts. Or three posts may be used, tepee-fashion, with the cloth draped around them. The umbrella blind is widely used, consisting merely of a stout umbrella fastened to a stake, with cloth siding attached to the umbrella and extending to the ground. Blinds should be of ample size, 5 or 6 feet high and with enough floor space to permit convenient manipulation of the camera. There should be a canvas camp stool inside for the photographer. It is essential that there be no flapping ends of cloth to scare the birds, and a neutral color is less disturbing to them than white. In photographing a nest, it is well to erect the blind some distance away and bring it toward the nest by easy stages, watching the birds' behavior the while.

BLINDS IN TREES. For birds that nest higher in trees, a roost in the tree itself, or better still in an adjoining tree, can serve the photographer. The camera should be on a level with or above the nest. The best device is probably a scaffolding that can be put up near the nest for the support of both camera and photographer. This means heavy wood, and is therefore not feasible unless the nest is near a road or other place that can be approached by motorcar.

One of the advantages of a blind is that it enables the photographer to gain an intimate view of the birds and their activities, so that even if his photographic work were not successful, he would still derive pleasure from his observations.

Remote control

Successful photographers disagree on the matter of remote control, some declaring that they never use this method, while others maintain that they never have to use a blind. Remote control consists of exposing the photographic film by pulling a thread or line attached to the trigger or by use of a cable release or an electric device. In tripping the shutter with a line, it is well to keep the line on a reel to avoid tangling, and to keep from running it around obstructions, as this delays the tripping action. It is well to pull the line almost taut, so that when a bird appears before the lens, you need give the cord only a light, steady pressure to trip the shutter. Do not pull the cord too hard, or you will damage the camera shutter; place the tripod solidly, or you may overturn camera and tripod when you pull.

The shutter can be tripped electrically by using one of the battery-operated solenoid-type coils that can be ordered at most camera stores. Electric trippers are convenient to use at any distance.

Some cameras, such as the Contax, are equipped with a shutter-release button in the center of the knob that winds the film. A picture is taken by depressing this button with the finger. However, the shutter may also be released from a distance by use of a cable release that is screwed into the threads inside the shutter-release button. The photographer needs only to press a plunger at the end of this cable to release the shutters. Such cables are available in varying lengths on order. I have one 20 feet long.

One of the disadvantages of remote control is that the operator has to go to the camera every time he wants to make another exposure. However, some of the miniature cameras, the Robot Royal, for instance, have spring motors that permit bursts of pictures at the rate of eight per second or the exposure of single units without winding the film each time.

Types of cameras

There is no one camera that is best for all purposes. My suggestion for the beginner is to experiment with whatever cameras there may be around his house before he determines to buy one especially for bird photography. When I first began to photograph birds, I found there were five cameras in my house that I could use, ranging from a box camera to a modern miniature. After you have experimented a while, you will have a better idea of the type of camera you want and the kind of photography you want to do. Everyone urges that the beginner buy a second-hand camera at first, and this is good advice, especially if the purchase is made from a store that has a reputation for reliability.

BOX CAMERAS. Nearly every family owns at least one box camera. They are easiest to operate; all you do is press the plunger and you have a picture. The lens of this type of camera is set at a fixed focus, so that all objects beyond six feet will be in focus. The lens is usually rated between f/11 and f/16, which means that its diameter is that proportion ($\frac{1}{11}$ or $\frac{1}{16}$) of its focal length, the latter being the distance between the lens and the film. However, at 6 feet, and with the short lens with which these cameras are usually equipped, a bird looks small. This fault may be remedied to some extent by purchasing a portrait attachment, at a cost of a dollar or so. This attachment permits objects within 3 feet to be photographed. The film, usually $2\frac{1}{4}$ by $3\frac{1}{4}$ or $3\frac{1}{4}$ by $4\frac{1}{4}$ inches, is large enough to make clear contact prints, and the picture can be enlarged if the bird seems small even after the portrait lens is used. Color film can also be used in these cameras. A disadvantage of the box camera is that its shape is awkward, and that you have to see the picture you are taking in a brilliant finder rather than in an accurate view finder or on a ground glass. The shutter speed is generally between $\frac{1}{40}$ and $\frac{1}{60}$ second, and this is not suitable for high-speed action photography. Because of its slow lens, the box camera cannot be used for taking snapshots in poor light. You may get photographs of birds at window feeding trays by hiding behind the curtains and snapping the birds at close range.

ROLL-FILM CAMERAS (Non-reflex). These have faster lenses than box cameras, and can be focused to give clearer pictures. They have a bellows or a helical-type lens mounting that permits the lens to be moved varying distances from the film to be exposed, and they usually have brilliant view finders that afford an approximate idea of the area that you are photographing, but do not show whether or not the picture will be in focus. They use roll film, as do the box cameras, and will fold into convenient space for carrying. They can be screwed onto tripods. The helical-type roll-film camera has a lens mounted in a rigid barrel which screws in and out for focusing. Film size is often $2\frac{1}{4}$ by $2\frac{1}{4}$ or $2\frac{1}{4}$ by $3\frac{1}{4}$ inches.

The most expensive models of folding or roll-film cameras have the finest high-speed lenses (f/3.5, for instance) and shutter speeds up to $\frac{1}{800}$ second. A window or peep-sight view finder and flash synchronization are standard on most current models. More expensive models are equipped with coupled range finders for speedy, accurate focusing. These better roll-film cameras, with their fast lenses, action-stopping shutter speeds, and coupled range finders, are quite suitable for the bird photographer. Their good lenses make possible critically sharp images suitable for big enlargements. Generally, it is not possible to secure telephoto or long-focus lenses for such cameras; this limits their use in taking pictures of birds at considerable distances, as on the far shore or waters. The Ansco Super Speedex, Super Ikonta, and Kodak Chevron are among the more expensive cameras in this class.

REFLEX CAMERAS. In this type of camera, the image seen through the lens is thrown by a mirror constructed into the camera onto a ground glass at the camera's top. This enables the photographer to view exactly the image that he will record. When the trigger is depressed, the mirror flips out of the way, the shutter opens, and the image is projected by the lens onto the negative. This type of camera shows the image right side up on the ground glass, and if it is a moving image, like a flying bird, the photographer can follow it up to the time of clicking the shutter. This camera has high shutter speeds, and a demountable lens board permits the use of many different lenses. It uses a film 2¼ by 2¼ or 3¼ by 4¼ inches, producing good contact prints or allowing excellent enlargements. You can buy an adapter if you want to make color slides. This camera is somewhat bulky and expensive, and has a noisy shutter. With this type of camera, you must focus with the lens wide open, and then stop the aperture down to the required size for exposure before snapping the picture. The Hasselblad is used by many nature photographers. Some, as the Exakta VX, are 35-mm.

The twin-lens camera, such as the Rolleiflex, has eliminated the latter inconvenience. These cameras have two lenses, one for focusing and the other to take the picture. You can set the lower lens to the required opening and leave it there, focusing with the upper lens wide open. To focus you merely adjust the focusing knob or lever until you get a sharp image on the viewing screen. What you see you get. These cameras are comparatively high-priced, because they have two lenses instead of one. They are easy to operate, but are square rather than flat, and hence awkward to carry. Most twin-lens reflex cameras put a dozen 2¼-by-2¼-inch negatives on each roll of film.

This camera does not have superfast lenses; f/2.8 is the fastest now available, and most models have f/3.5 or slower. Nor are the lenses interchangeable; hence you cannot shoot birds at a distance.

MINIATURE CAMERAS. The Leica and Contax are familiar examples of miniature cameras. These cameras have many advantages, but they are difficult to operate for best results. They use 35-millimeter film, producing 20 to 36 tiny negatives on a single roll. The film is inexpensive, therefore enabling the bird watcher to take interesting series of shots of bird behavior. The camera is small and easy to carry and to put into operation. However, these cameras cannot be focused accurately unless they are equipped with a coupled range finder or other similar device. The range finder indicates that the picture is in focus when there is a merging of the two images that are seen through it.

Although the lenses in miniature cameras are often remarkably fast, and the camera's short focal length gives depth of focus to make clear negatives, still the negative is so small that it is difficult to enlarge it successfully to a size of 10 by 12 inches or more. The grain of the film will be too marked in such enlargements unless one is able to master difficult techniques of development. The best pictures of birds can be taken when the camera is equipped with a telephoto lens, and these lenses are often as expensive as the camera itself. Although the camera is small, the accessories may be so numerous as to make a bulky bundle to carry. Miniatures take color transparencies that can be used for projection on a screen, direct viewing, or reproduction as color prints and enlargements. Every serious bird photographer should have a miniature camera in his possession eventually, although it is debatable whether he should start with such a camera as his main item of equipment.

My own miniature camera is a Contax that has an ultrafast f/1.5 lens and focal-plane shutters rated at a breath-taking $\frac{1}{1250}$ second. It has a coupled range finder for quick, accurate focusing, and can be fitted with a wide range of long-focus or telephoto lenses that will take bird pictures at great distances from their subjects. It takes cartridges affording 20 or 36 exposures in black and white or color. This camera can take excellent pictures under light conditions that would not be adequate for those equipped with slower lenses. If I want to take close-up views of birds, say small birds 13 inches away and big birds 30 inches away, I can use close-up or portrait lenses that may be purchased at relatively low prices. Such photography is rather unusual in occurrence and difficult in execution.

PRESS AND VIEW CAMERAS. These cameras possess ground-glass backs on which the picture is focused. The 12-exposure film pack or plateholder containing cut film is slipped into the place of the ground glass as that is taken out just before the picture is snapped. Some of these cameras are equipped with double-extension bellows that permit the lens to be projected far enough to allow close-ups of small birds and other small objects. Best results are obtained when the camera is used on a tripod, and some time may be required to focus the picture accurately. However, this may not be a matter of moment if the picture is taken of a stationary object such as a nest, which may be focused on in advance. The camera may use film 2¼ by 3¼ inches or larger, for example 4 by 5 inches, permitting big enlargements without the bother of fine-grain developing. An adapter can be used for color slides.

This type of camera is used by many professional photographers, and is possibly the best for the bird watcher who wants to secure fine photographs. A usable model can be found for most budgets. The typical press camera takes interchangeable lenses, has an open-frame sports finder for rapid shooting, and may have a focal-plane shutter with speeds up to $\frac{1}{1000}$ second. The standard lens is f/4.5 or f/4.7. The Graflex and Speed Graphic are cameras in this class.

Roger Tory Peterson, who says that he enjoys photography more than anything else he does with birds, tries to photograph ten new species each year. He uses a 4 x 5 revolving-back Auto-Graflex, and calls it the best all-around camera for wildlife work. It is equipped with a ten-inch Protar VII lens with an old-fashioned "compound shutter." This between-the-lens shutter is synchronized with a flash gun. He also uses a 4 x 5 Speed Graphic and a Leica.

Exposures

It is good advice for bird photographers to avoid taking pictures in strong sun, unless they are in the most exposed situations, as along a beach. This is because sun develops deep shadows and strong highlights that make a bird almost invisible against its background. The best light is that which comes from behind thin clouds. Some photographers use flash constantly, while others avoid it. Apparently it does not bother the birds, as they have been observed to continue their domestic duties without faltering in spite of a flash bulb being exploded in their faces. The beginner should probably work without flash until he becomes more experienced in photography. Eliot Porter, who took many of the photographs in *Land Birds of America*, uses electronic flash, in which electronic beams broken by a bird's flight set off the flash and the shutter. These beams intersect, and do not function until the bird crosses the point of intersection, which has been determined by the photographer as the point where it is in best focus. Such photography requires heavy equipment and arduous labor, and is for the professional rather than the amateur.

One advantage of synchronized flash equipment is that it permits work to be done on cloudy days or in the shade. This makes it possible to expose nests less as to time and sunlight than would be feasible if the photographer were waiting for adequate light during a period of overcast.

Correct exposure is not the problem that it used to be, what with exposure meters and modern film and printing papers. However, it is a prime problem that the bird photographer must continue to study, learning by trial and error and the experience of others.

Bird movies

Principles are similar in still shots and movie shots. Colored film is the epitome of bird photography as seen in WALT DISNEY's *Water Birds*, and in many amateurs' own footings. Birds are also easier to photograph with a movie camera, since a moving object is easier to photograph with an instrument adapted especially to that purpose. Moreover, most movie cameras will take telephoto lenses, necessary for distant shots and views of the smaller and more timid birds. Even if the bird photographer does not own a long-focus or telephoto lens, he can improvise by adding a binocular to the camera, so that one barrel serves as a camera lens and the other acts as a finder. This is a difficult operation, however, and has given me only indifferent results, although I know of others who have succeeded. You must be sure that the joining of the camera and the binocular is light-tight, that the camera does not move when it is held against the binocular, and that it is focused properly. The matter of light is difficult, for the binocular admits just enough light for the pupil of the eye to encompass, whereas the camera may need more or less than this amount of light.

Movie cameras with long-focus lenses should be used with a sturdy tripod; otherwise the pictures on the screen will jump. However, the stationary tripods are hindrances when photographing birds in flight, so gunstock mounts are desirable. These can be improvised, possibly from old military equipment, or can be bought.

Reading references

Photography Afield, by ORMAL I. SPRUNGMAN, The Stackpole Company, Harrisburg, Pennsylvania, 1951, 449 pp. and illustrations.

Bird Photography, by G. K. YEATES, Faber & Faber, London, 1946, 120 pp. plus 48 black-and-white plates.

How to Take Bird Pictures with Still and Movie Cameras, EASTMAN KODAK COMPANY, Rochester, New York, 1949, 16 pp.

The Art of Bird Photography, ERIC HOSKING and CYRIL NEWBERRY, Country Life Limited, London, 1948, Transatlantic Arts, Inc., New York, 103 pp., illustrated with photographs and sketches.

Nature and Camera, by OLIVER G. PIKE, The Focal Press, London and New York, 1943, 262 pp.

"Directory and Buying Guide" issue of *Photography Magazine*, 1954. This annual issue contains current information on cameras and photographic equipment.

chapter 16 / Why not join a bird club?

Bird watchers, especially beginners, have much to gain by joining a bird club. In fact, that is why bird clubs are formed, to help bird watchers pursue their interests as well as to help conserve bird life. There are bird clubs or societies on three levels, the local, the state or regional, and the national. They will be discussed in turn. A club that is called a "nature club" may devote an important or even major part of its program to birds.

Local bird clubs

I belong to a local bird club, the Summit Nature Club, whose headquarters is in Summit, New Jersey, and I suppose its program is typical of many. It has 150 members who participate in a very busy schedule, with one or more events every month. These events are lectures, illustrated by slides or motion pictures, field trips, and the Audubon screen tours. The seven lectures are given by persons of local or national reputation. Edwin Way Teale is down for a talk on "North with the Spring," and Maurice Broun lectures on "Hawk Mountain Highlights." Then there is a program of ten field trips to various parts of the state: to South Jersey ponds and Boonton Reservoir for ducks; a study of the club's own area for a Christmas census; to Tuckerton and Holgate for shore birds; to Troy Meadows for rails and bitterns. There are five lectures and films on the Audubon screen-tour circuit. This is a program sponsored by the National Audubon Society, from which local clubs can secure outstanding speakers and films if they guarantee certain minimum paid attendances.

This is a varied and full program, but it is not all. The members of the club engage in various study projects which seem exceptionally worth while. They are occupied with a thorough study of the area within a radius of five miles of the Summit Post Office. For ten years now they have conducted censuses the first week of each of the winter months of December through March, and thus have comparative data on the populations of species. They have organized 65 operators of feeding stations into a kind of bird intelligence network, so that they can let one another know of unusual visitors to any station.

This substantial program is available to members for only two dollars a year, and would not be possible, of course, without the unselfish work of enthusiasts. The field trips are conducted by experienced leaders. Any beginner who joins such a club will learn where to go to see birds, will gain experienced help in the identification of birds and the study of their habits, will enjoy fascinating talks and films by the foremost ornithologists, and will meet kindred spirits. Some local clubs also have publications, frequently quarterly or monthly mimeographed bulletins. Sometimes these are named after birds.

State and regional societies

There are various state and regional societies that have a broader scope than that of the strictly local club. They are of use to the bird watcher who may not live near a local bird club, or who wants to participate in conservation programs that require more than local resources to put into effect.

I belong to such an association, the New Jersey Audubon Society, and a brief description of its organization and program may suggest the nature of other, similar state or regional groups.

The New Jersey Audubon Society has some two thousand members, and goes back to 1911. It has a paid staff of two and is run by a board of directors composed of representatives of some of the outstanding bird and nature clubs in the state and of persons who are outstanding in ornithology in their own right. The Society maintains a headquarters in New Milford, and there it sells bird books, binoculars, and other supplies, even birdseed. Members are able to order this material by mail, and get it at a discount. At the headquarters there is a sanctuary, and there are plantings of shrubs and trees that attract birds, and typical birdhouses and feeding devices.

The Society issues to its members a printed quarterly news letter that informs them of Society activities, gives programs of field trips, presents news of conservation, and reports on bird life of the season in the five natural regions of the state. There is also a schedule of field trips for every month of the year except summer. These trips range from one end of the state to the other, so that members can view representative forms of bird life at the best seasons. Several of these trips last over week ends, and are well organized and attended, five hundred persons sometimes participating. They include lectures and films as well as bird watching. The Society maintains two sanctuaries and takes a leading part in supporting conservation in the state, being able to bear considerable influence because of its large membership. Membership for ordinary members is three dollars a year.

There are many other groups of similar wide influence; the Massachusetts Audubon Society is the largest and best organized of the state Audubon societies, listing some seven thousand members and publishing an attractive magazine. Then there are various regional groups composed of more advanced bird watchers. In my area, for instance, are the Urner Ornithological Club of Newark, the Delaware Valley Ornithological Club of Philadelphia, and the Linnaean Society of New York City. These groups are com-

posed of people who have made many contributions to ornithological field records in their states, and who carry on specific
studies. The Urner group is to issue a check list of the birds of
New Jersey, and the Delaware Valley group has published in two
volumes Witmer Stone's *Bird Studies at Old Cape May*, an
ornithology of coastal New Jersey.

List of bird clubs

Following is a list of local and regional bird and nature clubs.
Most of these names were obtained from the National Audubon
Society, 1130 Fifth Avenue, New York, and are organizations that
were affiliated with the Society in 1955. Some of these clubs are
local groups, such as the Ridgewood Audubon Society in New
Jersey, and some are genuinely regional or state groups, such as
the New Jersey Audubon Society. However, it is impossible to
differentiate distinctly, because certain clubs that carry names indicating a wide membership or influence are actually small, local
groups. The best course for the beginner is to conduct his own
investigation of the organization in his area that interests him.

ALABAMA	
Birmingham	Birmingham Audubon Society
Montgomery	Montgomery Audubon Society

ARIZONA	
Phoenix	Maricopa Audubon Society
Tucson	Tucson Audubon Society

ARKANSAS	
Fort Smith	Fort Smith Audubon Society
Little Rock	Pulaski County Audubon Society

CALIFORNIA	
Berkeley	Golden Gate Audubon Society
Beverly Hills	California Audubon Society
Carmel	Monterey Peninsula Audubon Society

CALIFORNIA (*Continued*)

Laguna Beach	Nature Study Group
Long Beach	Agassiz Nature Club of Long Beach
Los Angeles	Los Angeles Audubon Society
Los Altos	Santa Clara Valley Audubon Society
Marysville	Yuba-Sutter Audubon Society
Modesto	Stanislaus County Wildlife Society
Monterey Park	Angelus Nature Club
Pasadena	Pasadena Audubon Society
Paso Robles	Paso Robles Audubon Society
Pomona	Pomona Valley Audubon Society
Redwood City	Sequoia Audubon Society
Sacramento	Sacramento Audubon Society
San Bernardino	San Bernardino Valley Audubon Society
San Diego	San Diego Audubon Society
	San Diego Society of Natural History
San Francisco	Golden Gate Audubon Society
San Luis Rey	Buena Vista Audubon Society
Santa Ana	Orange County Ornithological Society
Stockton	Stockton Audubon Society
Walnut Creek	Mt. Diablo Audubon Society
Whittier	Whittier Audubon Society

COLORADO

Colorado Springs	Aiken Ornithological Society
Denver	Colorado Bird Club

CONNECTICUT

Fairfield	Audubon Society of Connecticut
Greenwich	Greenwich Audubon Society
Hartford	The Hartford Bird Study Club, Inc.
Meriden	Meriden Nature Club
New Canaan	New Canaan Bird Protective Society
New Haven	The New Haven Bird Club, Inc.
New London	Ornithology Club of Connecticut College
Terryville	Terryville Natural History Club
Waterbury	The Waterbury Naturalists Club, Inc.
Westport	Westport Audubon Society

DELAWARE

Newark	The Newark Bird Club
Wilmington	Natural History Society of Delaware

DISTRICT OF COLUMBIA
Washington   Audubon Society of the District of Columbia, Inc.

FLORIDA
Cocoa	Indian River Audubon Society
Daytona Beach	Halifax River Bird Club
Fort Lauderdale	Broward County Audubon Society
Gulfport	Gulfport Garden and Bird Club
Jacksonville	Jacksonville Audubon Society
Key West	Monroe County Audubon Society
Miami	Tropical Audubon Society
Sanibel Island	Sanibel Captiva Audubon Society
St. Petersburg	St. Petersburg Audubon Society
Tampa	Tampa Bird Club
West Palm Beach	Audubon Society of the Everglades
Winter Park	Florida Audubon Society

GEORGIA
Atlanta	Atlanta Bird Club
	Georgia Ornithological Society
Dalton	Bird and Garden Club of Dalton
Emory University	Georgia Society of Naturalists
Milledgeville	Milledgeville Audubon Society
Rome	Floyd County Audubon Society
Savannah	Savannah Audubon Society

ILLINOIS
Champaign	Champaign County Audubon Club, Inc.
Chicago	Illinois Audubon Society
Danville	Vermillion County Audubon Society
Decatur	Decatur Audubon Society
Evanston	Evanston Bird Club
Freeport	Freeport Audubon Society
Rockford	Nature Study Society of Rockford
Springfield	Springfield Nature League
Wheaton	Wheaton Audubon Society

INDIANA
Evansville	Lida Edwards Audubon Society
Indianapolis	Indiana Audubon Society, Inc.
New Castle	Blue River Audubon Society
Richmond	Richmond Audubon and Nature Club

INDIANA (*Continued*)
South Bend   Audubon Naturalists of St. Joseph Valley
                              South Bend Audubon Society

IOWA
Cedar Falls   Cedar Falls Audubon Club
Davenport   Tri-City Bird Club
Des Moines   Des Moines Audubon Society
                              Iowa Ornithologists' Union
Dubuque   Dubuque Audubon Club
Waterloo   Waterloo Audubon Society

KANSAS
Mound City   Linn County Audubon Society
Topeka   Topeka Audubon Society
Wichita   Wichita Audubon Society

KENTUCKY
Henderson   Henderson Audubon Society
Lexington   Audubon Society of Kentucky
Louisville   Beckham Bird Club

LOUISIANA
Baton Rouge   Louisiana Ornithological Society
New Orleans   Orleans Audubon Society
Shreveport   Shreveport Society for Nature Study

MAINE
Augusta   Augusta Nature Club
Bangor   Bangor Bird Conservation Club, Inc.
Brunswick   Audubon Society of the State of Maine
Calais   Lincoln Bird Club
Lewiston   Stanton Bird Club

MARYLAND
Baltimore   Maryland Ornithological Society
                              Natural History Society of Maryland
Cumberland   Allegany County Bird Club

MASSACHUSETTS
Belmont   Belmont Bird Club

MASSACHUSETTS (*Continued*)

Boston	Massachusetts Audubon Society, Inc.
Brockton	Brockton Audubon Society
Brookline	Brookline Bird Club
Cambridge	Nuttall Ornithological Club
Lynn	Lynn Bird Club
Nantucket	Nantucket Bird Club
Salem	Essex County Ornithological Club
Springfield	Allen Bird Club
Worcester	Forbush Bird Club

MICHIGAN

Ann Arbor	Washtenaw Audubon Society
Dearborn	Michigan Audubon Society
Detroit	Detroit Audubon Society
Grand Rapids	Grand Rapids Audubon Society
Mount Pleasant	Chippewa Valley Bird Club

MINNESOTA

Albert Lea	Albert Lea Audubon Society
Duluth	Duluth Bird Club
Mankato	Mankato Audubon Society
Minneapolis	Minneapolis Audubon Society
	Minneapolis Bird Club
	Minnesota Bird Club
	Minnesota Ornithologists' Union
St. Cloud	St. Cloud Audubon Society
St. Paul	St. Paul Audubon Society

MISSISSIPPI

Laurel	Laurel Audubon Society

MISSOURI

Kansas City	Audubon Society of Missouri
	Burroughs Nature Club
St. Joseph	St. Joseph Audubon Society
St. Louis	St. Louis Audubon Society

MONTANA

Billings	Billings Audubon Society
Great Falls	Rainbow Bird Club

NEBRASKA
Lincoln   Lincoln Bird Club
                           Nebraska Ornithologists' Union
Omaha   Omaha Nature Study Club

NEVADA
Reno   Nevada Academy of Natural Sciences

NEW HAMPSHIRE
Hanover   Audubon Society of New Hampshire
Meriden   Meriden Bird Club

NEW JERSEY
Audubon   Audubon Wildlife Society
Chatham   The Chatham Nature Club
Hackensack   Hackensack Audubon Society
Montclair   Montclair Bird Club
Morristown   Morris Nature Club
Newton   Sussex County Nature Study Club
Newark   Urner Ornithological Club
New Milford   New Jersey Audubon Society
Plainfield   Watchung Nature Club
Ridgewood   Ridgewood Audubon Society
Summit   Summit Nature Club
Trenton   Trenton Naturalist Club
Westfield   Westfield Bird Club

NEW YORK
Albany   Dana Natural History Society
Amsterdam   Sassafras Bird Club
Bedford   Bedford Audubon Society
Binghamton   Naturalists' Club of the Triple Cities
Brooklyn   Brooklyn Bird Club
Buffalo   Buffalo Audubon Society
Elmira   Chemung Valley Audubon Society
Genesee   Genesee Ornithological Society
Geneva   Eaton Bird Club
Monticello   Sullivan County Audubon Society
New York   Linnaean Society of New York
Manhasset   Lyman Langdon Audubon Society
Pleasantville   Saw Mill River Audubon Society

NEW YORK (*Continued*)

Rhinebeck	Rhinebeck Bird Club
Rochester	Burroughs Audubon Nature Club
Scarsdale	Scarsdale Bird Club
Schenectady	Schenectady Bird Club
Staten Island	Staten Island Bird and Nature Club
Syracuse	Onondaga Audubon Society
Watertown	North Country Bird Club
Watkins Glen	Watkins-Montour Bird Club
West Nyack	Rockland Audubon Society

NORTH CAROLINA

Charlotte	Mecklenburg Audubon Club
Fayetteville	Fayetteville Audubon Club
Greensboro	Piedmont Bird Club
Raleigh	Carolina Bird Club
Salisbury	Salisbury Bird Club

OHIO

Athens	Athens Bird Club
Cincinnati	Audubon Society of Ohio
Cleveland	Cleveland Audubon Society
Columbus	Columbus Audubon Society
Cuyahoga Falls	Cuyahoga Falls Audubon Club
Dayton	Dayton Audubon Society
Marion	Burroughs Nature Study Club
Painesville	Blackbrook Audubon Society
Steubenville	Forest Audubon Club
Toledo	Toledo Naturalists' Association
Youngstown	Youngstown Nature Club

OKLAHOMA

Oklahoma City	Oklahoma City Audubon Society
	Oklahoma Ornithological Society
Tulsa	Tulsa Audubon Society

OREGON

Portland	Oregon Audubon Society

PENNSYLVANIA

Allentown	Lehigh Valley Bird Club
Ardmore	Bird Club of Philadelphia

PENNSYLVANIA (*Continued*)

Athens	Susquehanna Valley Audubon Society
Doylestown	Doylestown Nature Club
Lancaster	Lancaster County Bird Club
Norristown	Norristown Audubon Club
Palmerton	Palmerton Bird Club
Philadelphia	Delaware Valley Ornithological Club
	Pennypack Valley Bird Club
Pittsburgh	Audubon Society of Western Pennsylvania
Reading	Baird Ornithological Club
Scranton	Scranton Bird Club
Sewickley	Audubon Society of the Sewickley Valley
West Chester	West Chester Bird Club
Williamsport	Williamsport Nature Club
Wyncote	Wyncote Bird Club
York	York County Bird Club

RHODE ISLAND

Kingston	Little Rest Bird Club
Providence	Audubon Society of Rhode Island

SOUTH DAKOTA

Huron	Huron Bird Club
Sioux Falls	Sioux Falls Bird Club

TENNESSEE

Chattanooga	Chattanooga Audubon Society, Inc.
Nashville	Tennessee Ornithological Society

TEXAS

Amarillo	Texas Panhandle Audubon Society
Austin	Travis Audubon Society
Beaumont	East Texas Nature Club
Dallas	Dallas Nature Study Club
	Dallas Audubon Society
	Paisano Nature Club
El Paso	El Paso Audubon Society
Fort Worth	Fort Worth Audubon Society
Houston	Texas Ornithological Society
	Houston Outdoor Nature Club
Mission	Lower Rio Grande Valley Audubon Society
Tyler	Tyler Audubon Society

UTAH
Salt Lake City   Utah Audubon Society

VERMONT
Woodsville   Community Bird Club of Woodsville and Wells
                        River
Woodstock   Hartland Nature Club

VIRGINIA
Sweet Briar   Virginia Society of Ornithology

WASHINGTON
Olympia   Olympia Audubon Society
Seattle   Seattle Audubon Society
                       Pacific Northwest Bird and Mammal Society
Spokane   Spokane Bird Club

WEST VIRGINIA
Huntington   Huntington Bird Club
Wheeling   Brooks Bird Club

WISCONSIN
Appleton   Appleton Audubon Society
Green Bay   Green Bay Bird Club
Madison   Madison Audubon Society
                      Wisconsin Society for Ornithology, Inc.
Milwaukee   Milwaukee Audubon Society
Superior   Superior Audubon Society

HAWAII
Honolulu   Hawaii Audubon Society
                      Hui Manu Club

CANADA

BRITISH COLUMBIA
Vancouver   British Columbia Bird and Mammal Society

MANITOBA
Winnipeg   Natural History Society of Manitoba

ONTARIO	
Chatham	Kent Nature Club
Hamilton	Hamilton Nature Club
London	McIlwraith Ornithological Club
Ottawa	Ottawa Field Naturalists' Club
Port Arthur	Thunder Bay Field Naturalists' Club
Toronto	Federation of Ontario Naturalists
QUEBEC	
Montreal	Province of Quebec Society for the Protection of Birds, Inc.
Quebec	The Provancher Society of Natural History
SASKATCHEWAN	
Regina	Regina Natural History Society

National societies

There are also some societies of national scope that the bird watcher might be interested in joining. Generally they publish journals, hold annual meetings, and lend their prestige and weight of membership to the causes, scientific or conservation, that they espouse.

NATIONAL AUDUBON SOCIETY. The National Audubon Society is composed of some twenty thousand members. It maintains an attractive headquarters building at 1130 Fifth Avenue, New York. Its program includes the following services or activities:

Audubon Junior Clubs, in which more than ten million children in schools and youth groups have been enrolled since 1910; Audubon camps, for training adults in nature and conservation; Audubon screen tours, lectures and color motion pictures, which reach an audience of 500,000 a year in some two hundred cities; Audubon wildlife tours around Lake Okeechobee, Florida, and into the Everglades National Park, under the direction of trained naturalists; Audubon art tours, loan exhibits of original art by noted bird painters.

Also a service department, through which advice as to nature books, prints, bird cards, binoculars may be obtained and such items purchased; branches and affiliates in more than two hundred communities; research projects, especially for species threatened with extinction; a photo and film department, from which wildlife photographs and slides can be purchased and educational films rented; a public information department, which offers its services to members and furnishes press and broadcast media with information about nature and conservation.

Also publications, including *Audubon Magazine*, sent to all members; *Outdoors Illustrated*, adapted to school use; *Audubon Field Notes*, publishing results of bird watching, including seasonal reports and bird censuses. There are other publications for teachers and youth leaders.

Also sanctuaries, the Society's wardens patrolling about a million acres in various places in the United States; an annual meeting in New York, with accompanying field trips to nearby areas.

Membership costs five dollars for regular members, ten dollars for sustaining.

AMERICAN ORNITHOLOGISTS' UNION. The American Ornithologists' Union is another national organization. Since its organization in 1883, the Union has made its work the advancement of its members in ornithological science and the publication of a journal of ornithology and other works relating to that science. At the second meeting of the A.O.U. a committee was formed for the protection of North American birds and their eggs against wanton destruction. This committee was instrumental in founding the National Audubon Society. Today the A.O.U. does not take an active part in conservation movements, but rather tries to advance scientific knowledge about birds. However, it has recently revived its conservation committee, and promises action in this field.

There are some 2,500 members in the United States and Canada. Those who are most active are professional ornithologists, chiefly persons connected with museums. However, anyone can become a member by paying four dollars; he receives *associate membership* status. One cannot become a full *member* until he distinguishes himself in ornithology in some fashion, often by writing papers for the A.O.U.'s quarterly journal, *The Auk*. This class of full membership is limited to 200 persons.

Associate membership, which is all most amateur bird watchers can aspire to, means a subscription to *The Auk* and the privilege of attending the Union's annual meeting. These meetings are held in widely separated parts of the country in order to make it easier for members in different geographical areas to attend. A representative meeting might be attended by two hundred persons, last for four days, and consist of the reading of technical papers on various phases of ornithology. The session is concluded by a field trip.

Most bird watchers will find *The Auk* concerned with subjects too technical for their interest and the annual meetings too far removed from their homes. However, by joining they may be helped to advance in their knowledge to A.O.U. levels, and they will help support an organization that is devoted to the scientific details of bird lore. The A.O.U. has no permanent headquarters; its secretary is Harold F. Mayfield at 2557 Portsmouth Avenue, Toledo 13, Ohio.

WILSON ORNITHOLOGICAL CLUB. This is a somewhat national bird club of approximately 1,500 members, who pay three dollars a year to receive quarterly *The Wilson Bulletin* and to attend the club's annual meetings. These are generally held in the Middle West, but the gathering in 1954 was held at Cape May, New Jersey. The secretary is Phillips B. Street, Exton, Pennsylvania.

THE COOPER ORNITHOLOGICAL CLUB. Although rather regional in operation and membership, the Cooper Ornithological Club has a national interest because of the excellence of its bimonthly magazine, *The Condor*. It also occasionally publishes *Pacific Coast Avifauna*. There are two divisions to the club: the northern division, meeting in the Life Sciences Building at the University of California at Berkeley, and the southern division, holding sessions at the Los Angeles Museum of Science, History, and Art. Three dollars covers dues and subscription to *The Condor*. Communications should be addressed to C. V. Duff, Business Manager, 1922 Tamarind Avenue, Hollywood 28, California.

CONSERVATION GROUPS. There are many excellent groups concerned essentially with the conservation of bird life and other natural resources, and the bird watcher will become interested in lending his support to one or more of these. A list is published in the *Directory of Organizations and Officials Concerned with the Protection of Wildlife and Other Natural Resources,* compiled by the National Wildlife Federation, 232 Carroll Street, N.W., Washington 12, D.C., July 1, 1954. Such an organization is Hawk Mountain Sanctuary Association, whose headquarters is in New York City. It has stopped the slaughter of hawks and established a famous sanctuary along the hawks' flyway at one place in the mountains of eastern Pennsylvania. Its president is Mrs. C. N. Edge, and the director of its sanctuary is Maurice Broun, author of *Hawks Aloft.*

chapter 17 / How birds got their names

Before discussing how birds got their names, it may be desirable to look at the bird's structural development out of its geologic past. That will help us to understand why birds are today listed in a certain order in field guides and other books.

History of birds

Back in the mists of geologic time the reptiles inhabited the sea. At some time, a race of these serpents crawled out of the sea to live on land. Some of them spent only part of their time on land, and became amphibians, but others remained out of the water. Eventually there developed a ground-living, lizardlike reptile. For safety's sake it took to spending much of its time in the trees and bushes. After eons of jumping about from tree to tree, this scaled lizard began to develop the lighter skeletal structure of birds, with hollow bones, an air-cell system to make the body lighter, and a wing structure that developed from the constant flapping of its front legs. Gradually the creatures assumed feathers instead of scales and a higher blood temperature. For a time they retained a set of free fingers on their wings, relics of reptilian claws. Indeed, there exists in South America today a remarkable creature, the hoatzin, that is a curious link with the past. It is a bird that retains many reptilian features, including five fingers on the wings of the young. The earliest birds had many of these characteristics, including naked heads, broad flat tails, toothed beaks, but no horny bills.

The geologic history of birds has many gaps, but it has been established that birds stem from the arboreal orders of lizardlike reptiles. Probably the more cumbersome of the early birds spent their time on the ground, with the resultant loss of power to fly. Today flight is difficult with many water birds, and some have only a vestige of a wing. Also from the secondary ground phase developed the large flightless birds such as the ostrich, many of which gained extraordinary running ability.

Systematic classification

Birds are classified according to the system devised in the latter part of the eighteenth century by the Swedish naturalist Linnaeus. This system divides them first into large *orders*, within which individuals are related, particularly as to skeletal, muscular, or visceral structures. In other words, birds belonging to the same order are related by their internal characteristics, plus similarities in a few external characteristics such as arrangement of toes and number of tail feathers. In most of the books with which a bird student is concerned, the birds are grouped by their orders, and these orders are always arranged according to a specific historical rank. In this rank, the first birds in the book are those that are most closely related to their original ancestors, the reptiles. Thus, the Gaviidae or loons come first in the books. These are aquatic birds that are comparatively helpless on land, and seem to be very much the same kinds of birds as those whose fossil remains are found in the strata of the Miocene epoch, some thirty to forty million years ago. Their nests are crude, the eggs often being laid on a shelf in the open; their voices are also crude and unmusical.

The succeeding orders are arranged according to the amount of deviation from their reptilian origin, and end with the passerine, or perching birds. This order is large, containing more than half the entire number of species. It also contains those with the most complicated habits. Their song is best developed, their nervous systems are the most sensitive, and their senses of sight and hearing are the keenest.

The great orders of birds are further broken down into *families*. They are distinguished from one another by more detailed skeletal differences. The next smaller groups are distinguished by differences of bill, wing, tail, feet, and sometimes patterns of marking. Birds bearing similarities in these features belong to the same *genus*. *Species* differ from one another in size and color, or external characteristics. According to Mayr's definition, "Species are groups of actually (or potentially) interbreeding natural populations which are reproductively isolated from other such groups." *

Not all birds in these classifications are markedly separate and distinct from one another, for, as Spencer observed, evolution is a continuous change marked by successive differentiations and integrations. In this process there are frequently found birds that are so little different from one another that they have been put into *suborders, subfamilies, subgenera,* and *subspecies.* A subspecies, for instance, is sometimes defined as a geographical race that blends with other races of the same species. The song sparrows along the coast of New Jersey are grayer than those inland, and have been given a different name, Atlantic song sparrow. This is a subspecies. The differences between subspecies are sometimes well marked, but in other cases, as with the subspecies of flycatchers, the differences can be told only by an expert with the bird in hand and after careful examination of the skins in a museum.

Scientific names of birds

In addition to its common or vernacular name, you will find that the bird books give every bird a scientific name. This name

* Ernst Mayr, E. Gorton Linsley, and Robert L. Usinger, *Methods and Principles of Systematic Zoology,* McGraw-Hill Book Company, Inc., New York, 1953, p. 25.

is composed of two or three Latin or Greek words, and is often followed by a man's name, either enclosed in parentheses or not.

The first of these names places the bird in the proper genus. (The order and family in which the bird belongs are indicated at the beginning of the section of the book in which the related birds are treated.) The second name puts the bird in its proper species, and the third name, if there is one, in the subspecies. If a man's name follows, it indicates that he first classified and described the bird, either the species if there are no subspecies, or the subspecies if there are. If the man's name is placed in parentheses, it indicates that he described the species named, but did not place it in the genus in which it is now found. In other words, you will not find the original description in his works under the generic name given.

Let us see how this applies to our Northern blue jay. The bird is named Cyanocitta cristata bromia (Linnaeus). *Cyanocitta* refers to the color of the bird, being derived from the Greek *kyanos*, meaning "dark blue," and *citta* meaning "jay." *Cristata* comes from the Latin *cristatus*, meaning "crested." So long as this jay appeared to be the only species, it was known only by these two names. Then it was discovered that there were other species closely allied, but distinct. The Florida blue jay (not to be confused with the Florida jay) differed sufficiently from the blue jay found in the Northeast to warrant its establishment as a subspecies, to be known as Cyanocitta cristata cristata. Another kind of blue jay was found in the extreme southern part of Florida, south of the Everglades, and named Semple's blue jay, or Cyanocitta cristata semplei. With these discoveries, it was decided that the original blue jay could not be left with just two names, as that would indicate that it was the species, of which the other jays were subspecies. So the third name, *bromia*, meaning "boisterous," was added to equalize the rank of the three birds, showing that all three were subspecies. The name Linnaeus enclosed in parentheses means that although that famed scientist described the bird first, subsequent findings have altered his original classification.

The scientific nomenclature of birds is a continuing process, and as new species and subspecies have been discovered, confusing changes have taken place. However, scientists are constantly working toward that ideal of a perfect system wherein each creature has but one identification tag the world around which will mean the same thing to the bird watcher in Bombay that it does to the one in Boston.

Common or vernacular names

The beginner will find, so far as names of birds are concerned, that by far the most interesting study will be of the birds' common or vernacular names. Some species, especially those that range over large areas and have outstanding characteristics, will collect many names, sometimes more than a hundred, as in the case of the flicker. If a bird has a dramatic personality, a colorful coat, or striking structural or voice characteristics, it will pick up folk names that correspond to the characteristic that most impresses people in the regions where the bird wanders. For instance, the bobolink is named for its bubbling song heard in the Northeast in spring. In spring and fall it migrates through the Southern states, and there has earned the name of rice bird because of its depredations on the rice fields in the coastal regions. The more outstanding the bird, the greater its collection of names, especially when one adds various South American, Mexican, Canadian, Indian, and Eskimo names to the bird's appellations.

NAMES DERIVED FROM BIRDS' VOICES. Let us examine some of the ways in which these names arise from folklore and become permanent and familiar labels. Some of the names of birds derive from the sound of their voices or wings. Such names would be veery, the thrush whose clear descending notes echo its name; the killdeer, pewee, phoebe, chickadee. One bird announces itself by two name calls, the towhee or chewink. Some say the blue jay derives its name in this manner, while others say that "jay" stems from the Old French *gai*, which came from the Italian; later it became *geai*, with the g softened, and still later *j* was substituted for it. This name, of course, applies to the bird's bright feathers and jaunty manner. The dickcissel sits on a fence in the Middle West and utters its "dick-ciss-ciss-ciss" tiresomely. The grasshopper sparrow sounds its insect noise on hot, sunny days.

Cuckoo, flicker, pipit add to the list of birds that sound their own names. And whence came the name "shrike," which on the surface seems to lack significance? It stems from old Anglo-Saxon and Icelandic words, *scric* and *shrikja*, both of which refer to the shriek the bird makes just before pouncing on its prey. Its other common name, butcher-bird, refers to its habit of impaling its prey on a thorn before devouring it.

NAMES FROM ACTIONS. Another class of birds are named for things that they do. Some are called wagtails, because of the nervous habit of pumping their tails up and down or from side to side. The bittern (origin lost) is also known widely as the sun-gazer from its habit of freezing with beak pointed toward the sky, making both its lines and coloring conform to the pointed grasses in which it hides.

The petrel's name means "little peter," and derives from the experiences of St. Peter trying to walk upon the waters. Petrels flutter like swallows over the waves, dangling their legs and pattering their feet, so that they appear to walk upon the water. Limpkins limp, creepers creep, sandpipers pipe up and down the sands, woodpeckers tap the trees, oven-birds build nests that are open at the sides like an oven. Hummingbirds make the sound with their wings that gives them their name, but they are also known by flowery and unwieldy terms in Latin America, such as flower-peckers, flower-kissers, myrtle-suckers, tresses of the day star, and rays of the sun.

The shearwater's distinctive flight close to the crests of the waves prompted its name, while the cedar waxwing was so named because its wings are tipped with red that looks like sealing wax. The scissor-tailed flycatcher has a long divided tail that looks and operates like the blades of shears, and, like any flycatcher, it subsists largely upon insects that it captures by sorties from the terminal foliage of trees. The chimney swift lives in chimneys. The roadrunner of the West, whose running speed can equal a fast dog's, has several interesting names. It was once known as the churca, and was described as a kind of pheasant (which it somewhat resembles) with four feet, two pointing forward and two backward. Actually this was a clumsy attempt to describe the bird's toes, which are four to the foot and so arranged. This bird is also known as lizard-bird (it eats them), snake-killer, chaparral cock, cock of the desert. Lapwing is a curious name that stems from the Anglo-Saxon. It comes from the words *hleape* and *wince;* the former meant to turn about in running or flight, and the latter to waver, words suggestive of the bird's irregular flight.

The black-and-white warblers build nests using moss, as their Latin name, Mniotilta, implies, or feed upon insects that are active around moss. The parula warbler's name indicates that it is a "little parus" or titmouse, descriptive of the bird's habit of occasionally feeding by hanging upside down from terminal twigs, as does a titmouse or chickadee.

APPEARANCE AND NAMES. Many birds derive their names from their appearance. Obvious are those named from their colors, scarlet, black-and-white, lazuli, indigo, blue, painted this or that. Pintail ducks, grosbeaks, longspurs with their extended hind spurs, are all apparent. The kinglet is a small bird with a golden or ruby crown, as the case may be. The mourning warbler is a cheerful little soul that wears its lugubrious label because of a blue-gray hood. The oriole's name is not so obvious. It again indicates a color, however, as it comes from the Latin *aureolus,* meaning "golden." Lord Baltimore, the colors of whose house were yellow and black, was doubly honored by Linnaeus and Catesby, both of whom applied the name Baltimore to one of the species of oriole. "Redstart" means "red-tailed," from the Anglo-Saxon *roth-steort,* but our word "start," in the sense of "flash," seems very appropriate too. In Cuba it is called *candelita,* little torch.

The prothonotary warbler is a curious anomaly. The word is compounded of Greek and Latin, meaning first notary. Originally there was no *h* in the word; both Audubon and Wilson used "proto," and the dictionary gives "proto" as an alternative. The protonotary is a papal official who wears yellow robes and who keeps a registry of pontifical acts. The name was apparently first applied by Louisiana Creoles. The word "grebe" comes from the Breton "krib," meaning a comb. The grebes are characterized by protrusions on their heads that might with imagination have suggested combs. I like the colloquial name "hell-diver," because of the bird's ability not only to dive in an instant at a sign of danger, but also simply to sink out of sight with its neck upright like a periscope.

BIRDS NAMED FOR PLACES. Some birds are named for places, usually with inappropriate results, especially if the bird has a long range of migration. Take the Tennessee and Nashville warblers that breed in Canada and the northern tier of states, or the Cape May warbler that made Cape May famous, but for many years was not seen there at all. I have seen one or two there, and each spring and fall there are a few records now, but Alexander Wilson, who named the bird from a specimen taken by another man, never saw it in life. Audubon's specimens, also procured by others, as he never saw it in life, came from Philadelphia environs. Gmelin gave the bird its specific name after seeing a specimen taken on a boat off Jamaica by George Edwards and painted by him. It certainly seems to be a fugitive sort of resident to take its name from the southern tip of Jersey. The pheasant gets its name from the river Phasis in Colchis, whence it was brought to Greece. "Turkey" is a curious misnomer; originally imported to Spain from Mexico, the bird spread in Europe, and the population forgot its origin; the French called it the *coq d'Inde,* while others hazarded the guess that it came from Turkey.

Some birds, such as the pine warbler, derive their names from the type of habitat. These would include swamp birds of various kinds, field sparrow, seaside sparrow, and the like.

BIRDS NAMED FOR PERSONS. Interesting stories can be told about the birds that have been named for persons. During the 1860's it seemed to be a popular thing to name the dainty and colorful warblers for ladies, with pretty dedications. There are Grace's, Virginia's, and Lucy's warblers. Not all was smoothly accomplished in this field, however. MacGillivray's warbler is often called Tolmie's warbler in the West because it was so intended by the discoverer, J. K. Townsend. Audubon, who had received Townsend's specimens, rather highhandedly pinned the unhandy tag of MacGillivray to this warbler in order to honor a Scotch naturalist and collaborator of his who never visited our shores. Dr. Tolmie was a physician and factor for the Hudson's Bay Company who had been friendly and interested in the discoveries of our men of science.

Another such instance is that of the Lawrence's warbler. This was discovered in 1874 along the Passaic River in New Jersey by David B. Dickinson, once known as the "John Burroughs of New Jersey." Herold Herrick of the American Museum of Natural History took the specimen to have it classified, and being engaged to the daughter of Dr. Lawrence, another museum scientist, named the bird after her father instead of after Mr. Dickinson.

"Blackburnian" seems accidentally to have been a happier choice, for although this warbler was named after an Englishwoman, Mrs. Blackburn, who had no connection with our ornithology, but did have a good collection of stuffed birds, nevertheless the name seems appropriate for a colorful black, fiery orange, and white bird. There are many birds named after famous ornithologists and naturalists, both here and abroad, such as Audubon, Swainson, Townsend, Baird, Wilson, and lesser luminaries such as Bell, Bachman, Kirtland, and others whose interest was an inspiration to those who were making a lifetime occupation of ornithology.

There are a few less obvious names that have become attached to birds from more remote sources. Such, for instance, is the knot, named for ancient King Canute because of his supposed fancy for the bird as a tasty dish. Michael Drayton even wrote about it as follows:

The knot that called was Canutus bird of old
Of that great king of Danes, his name that still doth hold,
His appetite to please, that farre and neare was sought
For him (as some hath sayd) from Denmark hither brought.

This bird, being highly esteemed as food, was at one time netted and fattened before being slaughtered.

The martin was named for the Bishop of Tours of the fourteenth century, who is the patron saint of France. St. Martin's Day, or Martinmas, is November 11. In southern Europe this is a pleasant time of year, and is called St. Martin's summer, corresponding to our Indian summer.

SOURCES IN OTHER LANGUAGES. Many names stem from foreign or ancient languages, which in their original root described the bird well. "Loon" comes from the Icelandic word *lomr*, meaning a diver, or an awkward bird. "Godwit" really means "good wight"—good in the sense of good eating. Ben Jonson refers to it as excellent food. "Guillemot" stems from French and Breton words, *gwelan*, which means "gull," and *moette*, which means "sea mew." A merganser gets his name from Latin *mergus* and *anser*, the first meaning to "dip" or "plunge," and the second meaning "goose." "Mother Carey's chickens," another name for petrels, is an odd anglicization of *Madre Cara*, the mother of Jesus, to whom European sailors pray before a voyage. This fact has been generally lost sight of, and Mother Carey is sometimes thought of as a marine witch or a relative of Davy Jones.

"Cormorant" comes from a Latin name that signifies a marine or sea crow. Roy Bedichek, the Texas naturalist, resents the injustice that has been done to this bird by attaching to it names with sinister overtones, erroneously implying a relationship to the voracious raven. He points out in his book, *Adventures with a Texas Naturalist*, that the cormorant was known to the Druids as a bird of ill omen. He would emphasize the more cheerful Oriental attitude toward these birds, which the Chinese use in fishing, training them to catch fish and return them to the boat. A jaeger gets its name from a German word meaning "hunter"; and "pomarine," the specific name attached to one variety of this bird, means "nostrils covered or partly covered with scales." This word stems from *pomato-rhinces*, Greek words meaning "cover" and "nose." "Duck" has many counterparts in many languages, all meaning "to duck, to dive, to stoop."

MISTAKEN NOTIONS. Once in a while a name will be bestowed upon a hapless bird in a mistaken notion of the bird's real personality or because of an ancient superstition, and this name will cling, reminding us of old country ways and beliefs. Such, for instance, is the family name of Caprimulgidae for the goatsuckers. Shepherds in Europe once thought that these birds came in the night and milked their herds of goats, and the birds have been stuck with this name ever since. The Southern name of "bull-bat" possibly stems from the noise and flight antics of nighthawks at mating season. A booming sound is heard when a nighthawk checks its long, swift dive and swoops upward. This is made by air rushing over taut feathers of the partly closed wings. The Indians along the Connecticut River used to believe that this noise

was made by the Shad Spirit, announcing that the shad were
about to ascend the river. A great amount of needless persecution
of these birds arises from the erroneous name of nighthawk. Eggs
are often destroyed and the birds shot. The bird is not a hawk,
but subsists on insects. "Brant" is a corruption of an old word,
brent, which contained the meaning "burnt," having nothing in
particular to do with the species of goose.

Reading references

Life Histories, by ARTHUR CLEVELAND BENT and contributors,
United States National Museum Bulletins, Smithsonian Institution, Washington, D.C., 19 vols., 1919–53.

Handbook of Field and General Ornithology, by ELLIOTT
COUES, Macmillan, 1896, 342 pp. A manual of the structure and
classification of birds.

What's In a Bird's Name, by ALAN DEVOE, *Audubon Magazine*, July–August, 1950, Vol. 52, No. 4, pp. 218–219, et seq.

The Origin of Birds, by GERHARD HEILMANN, D. Appleton and
Company, New York, 1927, 210 pp.

*An Adventure in Etymology, Part II, The Meaning in Birds'
Names*, by ERNEST INGERSOLL, *The Scientific Monthly*, Vol. 35,
September, 1937.

Methods and Principles of Systematic Zoology, by ERNST
MAYR, E. GORTON LINSLEY, and ROBERT L. USINGER, McGraw-
Hill Book Company, Inc., New York, 1953.

A Dictionary of Birds, by ALFRED NEWTON, ET AL., Adam &
Charles Black, London, 1893–96, 1088 pp.

A History of Birds, by W. P. PYCRAFT, Methuen & Co., London,
1910, 458 pp.

chapter 18 / Some famous bird watchers

Bird watchers will want to know of some others who have preceded them and who have contributed notably to the science. Everyone knows the name of Audubon, but who was Townsend and who Pallas, and what did they do to make ornithology a more exact science? There follow brief biographies of a score or so of the famous bird watchers of this country and Europe; the list is not inclusive, nor are the biographies detailed; however, they may give the beginner some notion of the able scientists who have also participated in this activity and by so doing added to the knowledge of birds which he now enjoys.

AUDUBON, JOHN JAMES (1785–1851). The foremost ornithologist of his time, Audubon's character and personality have colored his reputation and impressed themselves on any estimate of him as a scientist or as an artist. Reared in France as the adopted son of his natural father and the latter's wife, Audubon showed an early interest in drawing birds. He came to America and settled in the environs of Philadelphia in 1803, but showed no aptitude for any of his business ventures, which included operating a lead mine and running general stores in Kentucky. While his partner tended the stores, Audubon was likely to be found exploring the wilderness and painting the creatures he found there. During these ventures in Kentucky, he met scientific men and others, who became interested in his sketches. His irresponsibility led to the publication of some sketches of birds and fish he had invented, and this lack of accuracy affected some of the rest of his work. Once he really became absorbed in the business of illustrating wildlife in America, he traveled about sketching what he saw and paying his way by painting portraits and teaching.

While in Philadelphia to find a publisher for his paintings of birds, he was encouraged to seek an outlet in Europe, where, it was felt, there would be more interest in scientific findings. His reception was most enthusiastic in Edinburgh, and work was started there, and later continued in London, on the plates for his *Birds of America*. In order to publish these, he had to spend considerable time selling subscriptions to the forthcoming work. The engraver, Robert Havell, Jr., worked on the plates for eleven years. The first part of the elephant folio was issued in 1827, and was finished in 1838. In 1830 Audubon started writing the text for the *Birds of America*, which he called the *Ornithological Biography*. It ran to five volumes and occupied many years of work. The fifth and last volume of this was published in 1839.

In 1831 Audubon returned to America with a greatly enhanced reputation as an ornithologist. He met John Bachman of South Carolina, with whom he formed a great friendship, cemented by the marriage of two of Audubon's sons to two daughters of Bachman. The men collaborated in *Viviparous Quadrupeds of North America*, the publication of which took several years and was not finished until after Audubon's death.

Audubon's relations with Alexander Wilson, his rival for foremost position in American ornithology, were not too happy. They were marked by professional jealousy and accusations of plagiarism, but in his later years Audubon mellowed and liked to encourage younger men in the field. Any estimate of him as a scientist must take into account his inaccuracies and his reliance upon his collaborators, William MacGillivray and Bachman, for the scientific details of his work. He loved the outdoor, artistic, and literary aspects of his work. His birds were dramatized by action poses, sometimes to the point of being exaggerated and strained, but the fact remains that his contribution was more complete than that of any of his contemporaries, because of his wider travels and observations, and because of his use of species he never saw in life. His style was literary and his artistry excellent. Also it must be said that some of his inaccuracies arose from a lack of the kind of equipment that became available for subsequent scientists, such as field glasses and binoculars with which to examine birds in treetops. His omissions and confusion about successive plumages of birds were the result of the fact that so little examination had been made into these questions. It took many years of research to uncover and relate these matters.

With MacGillivray he also wrote the *Synopsis of the Birds of North America,* and kept many journals and diaries. He also issued a smaller edition of the *Birds of America.*

BACHMAN, JOHN (1790–1874). This close friend and collaborator of John James Audubon was a person of many talents and interests. His training, after a brief period of teaching, prepared him for the ministry, and he was ordained in 1814 as a Lutheran. The following year he was called to St. John's in Charleston, South Carolina, and there he built himself a distinguished career, marked by his humanitarianism toward the Negro.

It was here that his early interest in natural history really came to fruition, furthered by an acquaintance with Wilson and other early scientists in Philadelphia. It was given great impetus by a visit from Audubon in 1831, which led to their collaboration in *The Viviparous Quadrupeds of North America.* His contribution to the work was not only the collection of specimens, but much of the descriptive and editorial work. His interests extended to agriculture and botany. Bachman collected many specimens of birds in the Southern states for Audubon's use. Bachman's warbler and Bachman's pine woods sparrow are named after this early bird watcher.

BAIRD, SPENCER FULLERTON (1823–1887). This famous founder of the "Baird School" of ornithology, renowned for its emphasis upon accuracy, became interested in birds at an early age, and with his brother undertook intensive investigations and collections of specimens in his home state of Pennsylvania. He studied and taught natural history at Dickinson College, Carlisle, Pennsylvania, using a systematic method of field study in botany and zoology. He gained the interest and encouragement of Audubon.

After many years of work at the Smithsonian Institution as an assistant secretary, he became the secretary, and under his direction the collections became so enlarged and were being added to so steadily that in 1879 Congress authorized a building to house them. In 1871 Baird became head of the United States Commission of Fish and Fisheries, and devoted considerable time without recompense to furthering knowledge of ichthyology and the protection of fish in particular. The study center at Woods Hole, Massachusetts, which has become so famous for its oceanographic researches, was the headquarters for this activity.

Baird was particularly noted for the accuracy and detail of his descriptions and for establishing the theory that natural barriers helped bring about evolutionary changes in forms.

There are more than one thousand titles in his writings, among which are the following: *Catalogue of North American Birds; Review of American Birds; North American Reptiles*, in collaboration with Charles Girard; *Catalogue of North American Mammals*, and *A History of North American Birds*, with Ridgway and Brewer. He gave his name to Baird's sandpiper.

BARTRAM, WILLIAM (1739–1823). The son of John Bartram, the botanist, William was born in Pennsylvania and inherited his father's interest in plants. However, he had more diverse interests, which included the study of birds, to some of which he gave names, and specimens of which he sent to George Edwards and others in England. His main work was the *Catalogue of the Birds of North America*, in which he listed 215 species with notes on such matters as song, migration, nesting, and the like. He traveled more extensively than his father, and wrote accounts of his journeys. He was the first native American scientific ornithologist, and was the tutor and encourager of Alexander Wilson. He gave his name to Bartram's sandpiper, which was later called the upland plover, and is now known as the upland sandpiper.

BREWER, THOMAS MAYO (1814–1880). As so many ornithologists seem to have done, Brewer studied medicine and practiced for a while, until he gave up medicine in order to write and enter into the publishing business. Though most of his time was spent in the Boston area, he met or corresponded with many scientists. He knew Audubon and contributed some information to his *Birds of America*. He published a smaller edition of Wilson's *Ornithology*, a notable achievement because the larger editions of Wilson and Audubon had hitherto been too expensive for the average purse. He wrote many papers for the *Proceedings* of the Boston Society of Natural History, which he had joined as a young man. His particular contribution to ornithology was his *North American Oology*, published by the Smithsonian in 1857, in which were reproductions in color of eggs of the birds with full descriptions of the life histories and breeding habits. This publication was shortly abandoned, however, because of the great cost of the plates. Brewer also collaborated with Baird and Ridgway in the *History of North American Birds*. Brewer's blackbird owes its name to this pioneer ornithologist.

BURROUGHS, JOHN (1837–1921). A native of the Catskills, Burroughs was a prolific writer and sage of the hill country. For a time he taught school, studied medicine, and worked for the Government in Washington, where he became a close friend of Walt Whitman, even accompanying him on some of his hospital rounds.

In 1865 appeared his first nature essay in the *Atlantic*, to be followed by a long list of nature books and essays, the latter being a form of literature which he popularized with the American public. In 1873 he returned to his section of New York State to devote himself to the study of nature and to writing about his observations, though he frequently left home to travel. He was a member of the famous Harriman expedition to Alaska, which included many well-known ornithologists among its scientists. He camped in the Yellowstone with Theodore Roosevelt and in the Yosemite with John Muir. After a time he ceased writing in the purely lyrical vein about nature, and gave his attention to the more scientific side, although he always preferred to study in the field rather than in the laboratory.

Some of his titles are: *Wake Robin, Winter Sunshine, Birds and Poets, Locusts and Wild Honey, Leaf and Tendril.*

CATESBY, MARK (*circa* 1679–1749). A native Englishman, Catesby received some training in natural history in London, and first visited America in 1712. He remained in Virginia for seven years, collecting plants and seeds to send back to England. He was enthusiastic about introducing American trees and shrubs into Europe. His second expedition, begun in 1722, lasted four years and had as its purpose the study of the natural history of Florida, Georgia, Carolina, and the Bahama Islands. After returning to England from this trip, Catesby learned to etch, and undertook his monumental work, *The Natural History of Carolina, Florida, and the Bahama Islands,* which he published in large folio over a period of seventeen years. It consisted of two volumes and an appendix. The text was in French as well as English, and he illustrated the works with more than two hundred plates which he etched from his own paintings, directing the coloring of the first copies himself. He was also interested in the migration of birds and delivered a paper on the subject before the Royal Society, to which he had been elected in 1733.

CHAPMAN, FRANK MICHLER (1864–1945). Born in Englewood, New Jersey, Chapman interested himself when employed in a bank in New York by spending his lunch hours on a corner of Fourteenth Street, trying to identify the feathers of native birds on women's headgear. He listed 40 different species. He started to work for the American Museum of Natural History in 1886, and became curator of ornithology in 1908, holding this post for more than a generation. He has been credited with creating at the museum "the ornithological center of the universe." Chapman held that "if our studies of birds have no bearing on the progress and welfare of mankind, they are futile." His writing did much to popularize this study, and his *Handbook of Birds of Eastern North America*, first published in 1895, was standard until the 1940s. Other works by Chapman are *A Color Key to North American Birds*, 1903; *Camps and Cruises of an Ornithologist*, 1908; *My Tropical Air Castle*, 1929; *Autobiography of a Bird Lover*, 1933. He was the editor and founder of *Bird-Lore*, publication of the National Audubon Society that is now called *Audubon Magazine*.

COUES, ELLIOTT (1842–1899). A native of New Hampshire, this noted ornithological systematist studied medicine at Columbian (George Washington) University, where he also lectured. He was assistant surgeon in the United States Army. He was chiefly noted for his introduction of the botanical "key system" into the science of ornithology in his *Key to the North American Birds*. He published over five hundred titles. He was a founder of the American Ornithologists' Union, and was an associate editor of *The Auk*. He was also editor of *The Osprey*, another ornithological magazine. His wide interests included mammalogy. He served on the United States Northern Boundary Commission and the United States Geologic and Geographic Survey of Territories, whose publications he edited. His scientific researches have earned him an eminent position in the realm of ornithology, and his opinions are constantly quoted in current literature on the subject.

EDWARDS, GEORGE (1694–1773). This man has been called "the father of British ornithology," and is important to American ornithology because of the great amount of pioneer work he performed on American birds, though he never visited America. He was advised in this respect and also in the art of engraving by Catesby, and he was the recipient of many specimens of American birds from such contributors as the Bartrams. Having some wealthy patrons, he was able to publish four volumes of the *Natural History of Uncommon Birds* between 1743 and 1751. Fifty-seven American species were included in this work, whose plates he engraved and colored himself. He was a painstaking artist, albeit rather lifeless; he was most careful in his descriptions and recorded where he had seen a bird or from whom he had received his specimens. He traveled widely and tried, as far as possible, to see in life the birds he described, but he lacked Catesby's advantage of having seen in life the American species.

From 1758 to 1764 he was publishing *Gleanings of Natural History*, a work that included mammals as well as birds and was an extension of his earlier work. He worked prolifically, producing 900 drawings of birds and mammals.

FORBUSH, EDWARD HOWE (1858–1929). A native of Massachusetts, where most of his work was accomplished, Forbush's two greatest contributions to ornithology were his efforts to educate the public to the economy of birds and their protection, and the three-volume work published in 1925–29, *The Birds of Massachusetts and Other New England States*. This work is really wider in scope than would appear from the title, covering the northeastern United States. Louis Agassiz Fuertes and Allan Brooks were the illustrators. Bird ecology was given great impetus by his work for Massachusetts on the control of the gypsy moth; thereafter he wrote and lectured on the value of birds as destroyers of harmful insects.

Other titles include *Useful Birds and Their Protection*, 1907, and *A History of the Game Birds, Wild Fowl, and Shore Birds*, 1912. He was a distinguished member of the American Ornithologists' Union, a founder and president of the Massachusetts Audubon Society, president of the Northeastern Bird Banding Association and of the Federated Bird Clubs of New England. He also worked with and for the National Association of Audubon Societies.

FORSTER, JOHANN REINHOLD (1729–1798). A German who had been trained as a minister, Forster was also a mathematician. He had a great interest in natural science, and in his *Account of the Birds Sent from Hudson's Bay* he described many species new to the American list, including the black-poll warbler, the Hudsonian curlew, and the white-throated sparrow. He also published a *Catalogue of North American Animals*, and *Directions for Collecting, Preserving, and Transporting All Kinds of Natural History Curiosities*. The latter was a book much needed at a time when so many explorations and expeditions were under way with specimens being sent to Europe for classification. Forster's son Georg went with him on Cook's second voyage around the world. Forster taught in England for a time, and visited Russia to inspect some colonies along the Volga. He was a friend of Thomas Pennant, the English naturalist.

FUERTES, LOUIS AGASSIZ (1874–1927). Fuertes determined to be a bird painter when he was only fourteen. He was encouraged to pursue his career by Elliott Coues, who had seen some of his paintings. His first expedition took him to Florida in 1898. In 1899 he was with the Harriman expedition to Alaska; other travels took him to Texas, New Mexico, the Bahamas, the Pacific Coast, Saskatchewan, the Canadian Rockies, and South America. From 1924 to 1927 he was lecturer in ornithology at Cornell. On his death he left a very large collection of fine skins of birds, and more than a thousand sketches. His concentration in the field was so intense that his memory of the birds he had seen was phenomenal, and he could at any time sketch with great fidelity a bird he had seen many years before. He was a famed illustrator of the best-known bird books that appeared just before the turn of the century up to the time of his death in a grade-crossing accident.

LATHAM, JOHN (1740–1837). An English ornithologist who first described many American species, among them the sooty shearwater, white pelican, least bittern, dickcissel, great horned owl, song sparrow, swamp sparrow, vesper sparrow, sharp-tailed sparrow. Elliott Coues said of him that he was one of the six great names of eighteenth-century ornithology, the others being Catesby, Edwards, Forster, Pennant, and Bartram.

Another medically trained man who practiced, Latham knew and corresponded with leading scientists. His titles include the following: *General Synopsis of Birds*, in three volumes with 106 plates of his own, published in 1785, with supplementary work done later; *Index Ornithologicus*, two volumes, 1790, written in Latin; *General History of Birds*, a ten-volume work with an index on birds of the world, published from 1821 to 1828, his best-known and most comprehensive work, with 193 color plates of his own work.

LINNAEUS, CAROLUS, the Latinized version of Carl von Linné, (1707–1778). Conversant with several sciences, he was chiefly known as a botanist. His great fame rests upon the fact that he devised the "binomial system" of nomenclature, whereby every living creature and plant is known the world over by its own particular scientific name and can readily be recognized anywhere. He was born in Sweden and attended school and taught at Upsala. His works include *Flora Lapponica*, 1737, the scientific results of the exploration of Lapland in 1732; and *Systema Natura*, 1737, in which he set forth the principles of nomenclature. He traveled a great deal, was a practicing physician, and was issued a patent of nobility by the King of Sweden in 1761.

NUTTALL, THOMAS (1786–1859). The fame of this man rests upon his endeavors in two fields of science, botany and ornithology. English born, he came to Philadelphia as a young man and was a protégé of Benjamin Barton, the botanist. He accompanied many expeditions through America in search of plants. From 1822 he was for ten years curator of the Botanical Garden of Harvard University, and while he was in Cambridge his interest was directed toward ornithology. His two publications on the subject of birds were *A Manual of the Ornithology of the United States and Canada,* and a paper, "Remarks and Inquiries Concerning the Birds of Massachusetts." The first of these was much in demand, as the expensive folios of Audubon and Wilson were beyond the reach of the average person and were unwieldy to use. He recorded bird songs by the syllabic method. His interests also included mineralogy, shells, and geology. In 1834 he resigned his position in Cambridge to accompany the Wyeth expedition to the mouth of the Columbia River, another member of this expedition being J. K. Townsend, also an ornithologist. In 1842 he returned to England to live on an estate he had inherited, and devoted the remainder of his life to horticulture.

PALLAS, PETER SIMON (1741–1811). A German naturalist of great versatility, a student of medicine, and a traveler, Pallas first went to Russia upon the invitation of Catherine II to become Professor of Natural History at the Imperial Academy of Science at St. Petersburg. He was the naturalist on the expedition through southeast Russia and Siberia that Gmelin accompanied, and which lasted for six years. In 1812 he published three volumes about the accomplishments of the expedition. He described many birds of the Far North. Under the patronage of the Russian Empress, he lived and worked for many years in the Crimea, with his attention centered upon botany. He is often mentioned in bird manuals as having first classified some of the birds.

PENNANT, THOMAS (1726–1798). A scientist of broad interests, this Englishman's main contributions to ornithology were contained in a book, *Arctic Zoology*, two volumes describing 426 birds and some mammals, published 1784–85. This book was important to the development of American ornithology. He also wrote a pamphlet entitled "The Genera of Birds," 1773. Although his work contains some inaccuracies, nevertheless it was a valuable contribution to the ornithology of the time. He received specimens of American birds from Bartram, among others.

RIDGWAY, ROBERT (1850–1929). This distinguished ornithologist made a great many contributions to the science, more particularly to the technical side. He started on his career at the age of nine, mixing his own gunpowder and paints for shooting and delineating specimens. At seventeen he went on an expedition at the recommendation of Baird. He succeeded Baird at the Smithsonian in the care of the bird specimens, and in 1880 became curator of birds for the United States National Museum. He was one of the founders and a president of the American Ornithologists' Union, and he was particularly concerned with the committee on nomenclature and classification, which drew up the standard "Check-list." He went on many expeditions, including the Harriman expedition to Alaska. His publications include *Birds of North and Middle America*, eight volumes, 1901–19, and two more volumes he left nearly completed at his death; *Color Standards and Nomenclature*, 1886, 1912; *A History of North American Birds*, the *Land Birds* in three volumes appearing in 1874 and the *Water Birds of North America*, two volumes, in 1884, this work being written in collaboration with Baird and Brewer; *A Manual of North American Birds*, 1887, 1896; *The Hummingbirds*, 1892; *The Birds of Illinois*, two volumes, 1887–95. The first of these works was a tremendous accomplishment in systematic ornithology. Despite his position as foremost ornithologist of his day, he was innately shy, and served as president of the A.O.U. only on condition that he would not have to preside at meetings. Yet his personality was warm, and he was able to appreciate the beauty as well as the technical aspects of the scientific research in which he was engaged.

TOWNSEND, JOHN KIRK (1809–1851). A Philadelphian of Quaker stock, Townsend early developed an interest in birds, and became an excellent collector. One specimen, called "Townsend's bunting" by Audubon, is unique, and is preserved at the U.S. National Museum. At twenty-five he went with Nuttall on the Wyeth expedition to the Columbia River. He traveled extensively in the Northwestern states, and was a surgeon at Fort Vancouver. While in this region and later in the Pacific he collected specimens, many of which found their way to Audubon. He first discovered and described many birds from the Northwest, some of which appeared in Audubon's *Birds of America*, while some of his descriptions of mammals appeared in the *Viviparous Quadrupeds*. Among his publications was the first volume of a proposed work, *Ornithology of the United States of North America*, 1840. However, the appearance of a smaller edition of Audubon's *Birds of America*, and the poor support for his project, prevented his continuance of the work. In 1842 he was collecting and mounting specimens for the forerunner of the National Museum. Later he studied dentistry. He planned another tour as naturalist aboard a naval vessel, but his poor health forced him to abandon that project, and he died soon afterward.

He wrote many articles for journals, and published *Narrative of a Journey Across the Rocky Mountains to the Columbia River*. Townsend's solitaire is a bird named after this noted Philadelphian.

WILSON, ALEXANDER (1766–1813). A would-be poet, born in Scotland, itinerant peddler and weaver, Wilson first came to America at the age of twenty-eight. He taught school and eventually came under the influence of William Bartram, who stimulated his natural interest in birds. In Bartram's library Wilson had access to good books on natural history, and soon he conceived his project for his *American Ornithology*. At first he tried to learn etching in emulation of his models, Catesby and Edwards, but soon gave over that part of the work to a professional. He would draw the figure which the engraver would put on a plate, and then Wilson would color the proof and some of the copies, most of that phase of the work being done again by a professional working after Wilson's models. He worked on *American Ornithology* from 1808 until his death, when he was in the midst of the eighth volume. George Ord completed this and wrote the ninth volume from Wilson's notes, as well as a biography of the ornithologist. Ord was Wilson's loyal supporter and spokesman in the unfortunate controversies with Audubon. In the text Wilson gave, in simple and charming prose, accounts of the birds as he had come upon them in their natural surroundings. Since he did not travel so much as Audubon, his scope was more limited, being confined to Eastern North America north of Florida. However, he recorded accurately whatever he saw and covered his area nearly completely, and he was held in high esteem by scientists. Like Audubon, Wilson had to sell subscriptions to his work, traveling by stage and afoot, before his volumes could be published. Wilson gave his name to a warbler and a thrush.

Reading references

Biographies of Members of the American Ornithologists' Union, by T. S. PALMER and OTHERS, reprinted from *The Auk*, 1884–1954, Washington, D.C., 1954, 630 pp.

Dictionary of American Biography, edited by ALLEN JOHNSON, published by Charles Scribner's Sons under the auspices of the American Council of Learned Societies, 1929.

History of American Ornithology before Audubon, by ELSA GUERDAM ALLEN, American Philosophical Society *Transactions*, Philadelphia, New Series, Vol. 41, Part 3, 1951.

Index

Abbé, Ernest, 88
Abbott, Charles C., 124
Accipiters, 35
Account of the Birds Sent from Hudson's Bay, Forster, 202
Acorns, 48, 83
Adventure in Etymology, An, Ingersoll, 195
Adventures with a Texas Naturalist, Bedichek, 193
African cattle egret, 118
Airplanes, 131–132
Airports, 11, 16, 22, 123–124, 131
Alabama, 5, 75
  bird clubs in, 171
Alaska, 199, 203, 205
Albert R. Brand Bird Song Foundation, 104
Album of Southern Birds, An, Grimes and Sprunt, 102
Alcids, 28, 120–122
Alder flycatcher, 156
Aldrich, John W., 102
Alexander, W. B., 99
Allen, Arthur A., 34, 41
Allen, Elsa Guerdam, 207
Allen, G. A., 96
Amadon, Dean, 98–99
American Bird Banding Association, 138
"American Bird Songs," Brand, 34
American bittern, 17, 21, 32
American crow, 34
American eagle, 114
American egret, 19–20, 32, 134
American eider, 122
American goldeneye, 20, 60, 121–122
American merganser, 20, 36
American Ornithologists' Union, 13, 106–107, 181–182, 201–202, 205–206
American Ornithology, Wilson, 207
American scoter, 118

American Song Birds, 104
American widgeon, 17, 20
American Wildlife and Plants, Martin *et al.*, 85
Andrews Point, 122
Annuals, seed-bearing, 82
"Anting," 158
Apple blossoms, 13, 77
  (*See also* Orchards)
Arctic, the, 13
Arctic loon, 123
Arctic tern, 140–141
Arctic Zoology, Pennant, 205
Arizona, bird clubs in, 171
Arizona and Its Bird Life, Brandt, 102
Arkansas, bird clubs in, 171
Arkansas kingbird, 60, 81
Army bird walk, 114–115
Art of Bird Photography, The, Hosking and Newberry, 167
Asbury Park, New Jersey, 121
Ash-throated flycatcher, 60
Atlantic, 199
Atlantic song sparrow, 186
Attracting Birds, McAtee, 84
Audubon, John James, 99, 138, 190–192, 206–207
  biography of, 196–197
Audubon Bird Guide, Pough, 2, 95, 97
Audubon Field Notes, 102, 181
Audubon Guide to Attracting Birds, Baker *et al.*, 72
Audubon Junior Clubs, 2, 180
Audubon Magazine, 4, 181
Audubon Nature Center, Greenwich, 43
Audubon Water Bird Guide, Pough, 2, 33, 95, 97, 141
Audubon's warbler, 79
Auk, razor-billed, 28, 120, 122
Auk, The, 181–182, 201

Haystacks, 16, 123
Headgear, 28
Headstrom, Richard, 104, 154
Heilmann, Gerhard, 195
Hell-divers (*see* Grebes)
Hemlocks, 16, 23, 49
Hermann Park, Houston, 21
Hermit thrush, 22, 76–80
Heronries, 19, 118, 134
Herons, 9, 17, 25–26, 33, 128–129, 143
  great blue, 20–21, 32, 120, 134, 142
  great gray, 138
  green, 17, 20–21, 120
  little blue, 20, 134
  Louisiana, 20, 134
  night (*see* Night heron)
Herrick, Herold, 192
Herring gull, 20–21, 122, 142
Hickey, Joseph J., 103
History of American Ornithology before Audubon, Allen, 207
History of Birds, A, Pycraft, 195
History of the Game Birds, Wild Fowl, and Shore Birds, A, Forbush, 202
History of North American Birds, Baird *et al.*, 198–199, 205
Hoatzin, 185
Holboell's grebe, 122
Holgate, New Jersey, 169
Holly, 19, 75, 79
Homes for Birds, Kalmbach and McAtee, 64*n.*, 72
Honeysuckle, 83
  bush, 74, 81
Hooded merganser, 20, 60
Hooded warbler, 156
Horned grebe, 21, 123
Horned lark, 11, 16–18, 22, 27, 121, 123–124, 156
Horsehair, 150–151
Hosking, Eric, 167
House finch, 60, 64
House sparrow, 33, 56–57, 60, 150–151
House wren, 35, 60, 64, 150–151, 156
  mating of, 141
Houston, Texas, 21
How to Know the Birds, Peterson, 97
How to Select Binoculars, 93
How to Study Birds, Smith, 103
How to Take Bird Pictures with Still and Movie Camera, 167

Huckleberries, 75, 80
Hudsonian curlew, 17, 202
Hummingbirds, 5, 18, 83, 101, 119, 156, 189
  foods eaten by, 42, 46
  nests of, 150, 152
Hummingbirds, The, Ridgway, 205
Hunting, 139, 147
Hurricanes, 133–134

Ibis, glossy, 118
  white, 116
  wood, 116
Iceland gull, 18, 121–122
Identification, of birds, 30–36, 95, 136
  of birds' nests, 154
Illinois, 148
  bird clubs in, 173
Independence, California, 150
Index Ornithologicus, Latham, 203
Indiana, bird clubs in, 173–174
Indigo bunting, 152
Ingersoll, Ernest, 195
Inland Bird-Banding Association, 148
Inland Bird-Banding News, 148
Insect repellent, 29
Insects, 29, 36, 39–42, 48, 57, 74–75, 84, 119–120, 202
  in nesting boxes, 63
Invalids, bird watching by, 8, 39
Iowa, 42, 102
  bird clubs in, 174
Ipswich sparrow, 17
Island Beach, New Jersey, 19, 115, 131
Ithaca, New York, 34

Jack, Anthony, 104
Jaegers, 17–18, 193
Japanese beetles, 41, 57
Jaques, Francis Lee, 103
Jays, 48, 61, 63, 101
  Florida, 187
  (*See also* Blue jay)
Jersey City, 20
Jewett, Stanley G., 102
Johnson, Allen, 207
Jonson, Ben, 193
Jourdain, F. C. R., 99
Juncos, 7, 38, 44, 46, 49, 55, 82
Juneberries, 75, 78
Juniper, 75–76

United States National Museum, 100–101, 205–206
Upland sandpiper, 22, 123–124
Urner, Charles A., 103, 114
Urner Ornithological Club, 114, 125, 170–171
Useful Birds and Their Protection, Forbush, 202
Usinger, Robert L., 186n., 195
Utah, bird clubs in, 179

Valley quail, 79–81
Van Tyne, Josselyn, 13
Veeries, 77–80, 188
Vermont, 133
  bird clubs in, 179
Vesper sparrow, 18
Violet-green swallow, 60, 64–66
Vireos, 18, 33, 36, 51, 63, 84, 101, 153–154
  red-eyed, 77–78, 80–81, 156
  warbling, 80
  white-eyed, 35, 76, 79, 113, 156
  yellow-throated, 113, 152
Virginia, 200
Virginia creeper, 75, 79
Virginia rail, 17, 21, 125, 156
Virginia's warbler, 191
Vitamins, 42, 48
Viviparous Quadrupeds of North America, Audubon and Bachman, 196–197, 206
Vultures, 26, 30, 115, 120

Wagtails, 101, 189
Wake Robin, Burroughs, 200
Walk, identification by, 31–32
Walkill River, 119–120
Walking, bird watching and, 5, 10, 111
  (*See also* Field trips)
Warbler trees, 22
Warblers, 6, 9, 17–18, 22, 25–26, 34–36, 84, 88, 113, 130–132
  Audubon, 79
  bay-breasted, 113, 130
  black-poll, 113, 202
  black-throated blue, 34
  black-throated green, 113, 149, 152
  black-and-white, 18, 22, 31, 113, 190
  Blackburnian, 22, 35, 113, 192

Warblers, blue-winged, 18
  Cape May, 22, 129, 191
  chestnut-sided, 22, 113, 156
  Connecticut, 130
  Grace's, 191
  hooded, 156
  Kentucky, 35
  Kirtland's, 13
  Lawrence's, 191–192
  Lucy's, 191
  MacGillivray's, 191
  magnolia, 22, 113, 156
  mourning, 190
  myrtle, 9, 18, 45, 57, 76, 113, 118, 129–130
  Nashville, 18, 125, 191
  nesting boxes for, 65
  palm, 31, 118
  parula, 18, 22, 113, 190
  pine, 18, 22, 113, 190
  prairie, 18
  prothonotary, 190
  Tennessee, 130, 191
  Tolmie's, 191
  Virginia's, 191
  Wilson's, 113, 207
  wood, 101
  worm-eating, 16
  yellow, 77, 130, 152, 154, 156
Warbling vireo, 80
Washington, D.C., 173, 183
Washington Monument, 130
Washington (state), 101, 179
  University of, 95, 102
Watching Birds, Fisher, 103
Watchung Mountain ridge, 22, 119, 135
Watchung Reservation, 21
Water for birds, 40, 45, 48, 50–52, 55
  (*See also* Bird baths)
Water Birds, Disney, 166
Water and Shore Birds of California, 95
Water thrush, 31
Wayne's clapper rail, 116
Weather, bird watching and, 24, 28
Weaver finch, 60
Wellfleet, Massachusetts, 18, 116, 124
West, the, 94–95, 100
  (*See also* names of states)
West Indies, 97, 133, 142

West Virginia, bird clubs in, 179
Westchester County, 21
Western Bird-Banding Association, 148
Western bluebird, 60, 65, 79, 81
Western flicker, 79–80
Western meadowlark, 20
Western sandpiper, 33
Western tanager, 38
Westfield Bird Club, 125
Wetmore, Alexander, 99
What's in a Bird's Name, Devoe, 195
Whip-poor-wills, 126, 134–135
Whistling swan, 21, 131
White-breasted nuthatch, 60, 142, 144
White-crowned sparrow, 81, 118
White-eyed towhee, 115
White-eyed vireo, 35, 76, 79, 113, 156
White ibis, 116
White-throated sparrow, 18, 78, 80–81, 118, 202
White-winged crossbill, 16, 18, 21, 23, 36, 49, 83
White-winged gull, 18
Whitman, Walt, 199
Widgeon, 17, 20
Wild cherries, 75–76n.
Wild ducks, 86
Wild turkey, 76, 79–80, 116
Wildlife Conservation, Gabrielson, 104
Wildlife Refuge, Florida, 17
Willets, 116
Wilson, Alexander, 190–191, 196–197, 199
   biography of, 206–207
Wilson Bulletin, The, 182
Wilson Ornithological Club, 11, 182
Wilson's petrel, 18, 117, 133, 193
Wilson's snipe, 17, 129
Wilson's thrush, 207
Wilson's warbler, 113, 207
Wind, 27–28
   protection of birds against, 70
Window-shelf feeders, 52
Windows, picture taking from, 159
Wings at My Window, Govan, 7, 104
Winter, bird watching in, 25, 27, 29
   birds seen in, 7, 15, 18–20, 22–23, 35, 120–125

Winter, food for, 41–49
   (*See also* Christmas counts)
"Winter reed birds," 124
Winter snipe (*see* Purple sandpiper)
Winter Sunshine, Burroughs, 200
Winter wren, 35
Wintergreen, 80
Wisconsin, bird clubs in, 179
Wisner, Edward M., 155
Witherby, H. F., 99
Wood duck, 21, 60, 64, 69–70, 121
Wood ibis, 116
Wood pewee, 9
Wood thrush, 6, 75, 77–78, 80, 142, 152, 156
Wood warbler, 101
Woodcocks, 9, 13, 131, 156
Woodpeckers, 6, 22, 30–31, 65, 84, 101, 189
   downy, 18, 38, 60, 142
   foods eaten by, 43, 44, 47–49, 76–77, 79–80
   golden-fronted, 60, 64
   hairy, 9, 18, 39, 43, 60
   Lewis', 77
   nesting boxes for, 64, 67, 69, 150
   photographing of, 159
   pileated, 26, 116, 125
   red-bellied, 22, 76–77, 79, 115–116, 122
   red-headed, 5, 26, 60, 64, 77–79, 81, 120
Woodpeckers' holes, 60, 65–66, 69
Woods Hole, Massachusetts, 198
Woodstock, Vermont, 133
Worm-eating warbler, 16
Worms, 37, 40, 48–49
Wren tit, 78–81
Wrens, 35–36, 65–66, 101, 151
   Bewick's, 60, 64–66
   Carolina, 9, 34–35, 60
   food of, 76, 79
   house, 35, 60, 64, 141, 150–151, 156
   marsh, 17, 21, 35–36, 156
   nesting boxes for, 64–66
   winter, 35
Wyeth expedition, 204, 206

Yard lists, 8–9
Yards, 18, 21, 126
Yeates, G. K., 167
Yellow warbler, 77, 130, 152, 154, 156

ABOUT THE AUTHOR Roger Barton's avocation, or hobby, is
birds—an interest which he shares with others through his
activities as president of the New Jersey Audubon Society
and through a weekly outdoor column which he writes
for the *Newark Sunday News*. He has always been interested in birds, and when he lived in Brooklyn as a boy, he
would go to Prospect Park early in the morning before
school to watch them. Today he spends most of his week
ends observing and making notes on birds and conducting
bird walks and bird-watching expeditions. He has made
many such trips in Canada and along the whole length of the
Atlantic Coast. Mr. Barton has been a newspaper reporter
and editor, an advertising account executive, and president
of his own advertising agency. During the war he was an intelligence and public relations officer and was awarded the
Legion of Merit. He finds time in his busy schedule as editor
of two magazines in the advertising field not only to increase
his knowledge of birds, but also to study other natural history subjects, especially flowers and insects.

NARSYON